Wayward Icelanders

Helgi Gunnlaugsson
&
John F. Galliher

Wayward Icelanders

*Punishment, Boundary Maintenance,
and the Creation of Crime*

The University of Wisconsin Press

The University of Wisconsin Press
2537 Daniels Street
Madison, Wisconsin 53718

3 Henrietta Street
London WC2E 8LU, England

Chapter 3, with the exception of the postscript, originally appeared in the *Law and Society Review* 20 (1986): 335–353 and is reprinted by permission of the Law and Society Association.

The section "Secret Policing in Iceland" in chapter 7 originally appeared as "The Secret Drug Police of Iceland," by Helgi Gunnlaugsson and John F. Galliher in *Undercover: Police Surveillance in Comparative Perspective,* ed. Cyrille Fijnaut and Gary Marx (The Hague: Kluwer Law International, 1995), pp. 235–247, and is reprinted by permission of Kluwer Law International.

Library of Congress Cataloging-in-Publication Data

Gunnlaugsson, Helgi.
    Wayward Icelanders : punishment, boundary maintenance, and the creation of
crime / Helgi Gunnlaugsson, John F. Galliher.
    184 pp.   cm.
    Includes bibliographical references and index.
    ISBN 0-299-16530-2 (cloth: alk. paper)
    ISBN 0-299-16534-5 (pbk.: alk. paper)
    1. Crime—Iceland—History.   2. Punishment—Iceland—History.   I. Galliher,
John F.   II. Title.
    HV7028.5.G86   2000
    364.94912—dc21   99-6442

To Kristín Hildur, Páll Fannar, and Elín Áslaug
—H. G.

To Jeanne, Dan, and Leigh
—J. F. G.

Contents

Tables

Graphs

Acknowledgments

Thanks are due Ronald Farrell, Þóroddur Bjarnason, Rannveig Þóris-dóttir, Ingi Rúnar Eðvarðsson, Jeanne Galliher, Albert Cohen, Patricia Morrow, William Skinner, Stephen Wieting, Kai Erikson, Richard Quinney, Erlendur Baldursson, Þorbjörn Broddason, Hildigunnur Ólafsdóttir, Pétur Þorsteinsson, Yngva Digernes, and Brent Myer, for assistance with this research. We also gratefully acknowledge support from the Icelandic Research Council, the Scandinavian Research Council for Criminology, and the Research Fund of the University of Iceland.

Wayward Icelanders

1
Looking for Nations with Little Crime

Criminologists have typically studied social situations where the greatest amount of crime occurs, but it can be argued that we can learn the most from studying social situations where little crime occurs. Nations with little crime must be considered if we take as our primary task the creation of knowledge of how crime can be prevented and if we want to determine the linkage of punishment to social structure, rather than the relationship between punishment and crime. Indeed, many have demonstrated that the amount of crime in a society does not allow one to predict the societal response or severity of punishment (Hagan et al., 1979; Myers, 1979–1980; Liska, 1987; Christie, 1993).

Previous Research in European Countries with Little Crime

Marshall Clinard's book on Switzerland, *Cities with Little Crime* (1978), is an exception to the general rule of criminological research focusing on societies with high levels of law violation. Yet there is some debate about whether Clinard's selection of Switzerland provided the best candidate for analysis of a low-crime society. The Danish criminologist Flemming Balvig (1988) argued that Clinard's focus on Switzerland as a relatively crime-free society was inappropriate. Balvig observed that Clinard judged Switzerland to be a nation with little crime by allowing his perspective as an American to dominate his judgment. "One might be justified in asking whether any American criminologist would not in fact reach the same conclusions no matter what other country was being studied" (Balvig, 1988: 18). According to Balvig, crime news in the Swiss press helps maintain this low-crime image. Swiss papers do not emphasize crime news in either the number or length or placement of articles (Clinard, 1978: 28–30). Switzerland, unlike Denmark, has no daily tabloids which trumpet the problem of crime; thus there is no challenge in the press to the established view that

Switzerland is a nation without crime. "In this way, the Swiss society affords proof that there is no natural relationship between the level of criminality and the volume of crime stories in the newspapers" (Balvig, 1988: 110). The type of crime coverage is, of course, merely an editorial decision.

Surveys of Zürich citizens show they typically feel traffic to be their most important problem of law violation (Balvig, 1988: 26). Thus in Switzerland, police view the prevention of traffic crimes as an important and prestigious law enforcement activity. The local press also gives great attention to traffic deaths. Swiss conviction statistics from the early 1970s indicate that convictions for traffic violations exceeded all other offenses. This high priority given to traffic violations by both the public and the police also helps to maintain the image of the nation as essentially crime free. But according to Balvig, victim surveys give a picture of the Swiss crime problem that is different from that in the press. Clinard cited a victim survey that found 2.5 percent of Zürich residents had been assaulted during the previous year, and he noted that 34 percent of households in Zürich had been the victims of one or more crimes during the previous year (Clinard, 1978: 67, 70). Consequently it seemed curious to Balvig that Clinard has defined Switzerland as being highly unusual as a land with little crime.

Between 1975 and 1983 the Swiss police force grew by one-third, primarily to fight the drug problem. Arrests for drug offenses rose 161 percent during the period 1975–1983. In 1983, 72 percent of all drug offenses involved consumption; 5 percent, sales; and 23 percent, both (Balvig, 1988: 95). "Police in the Canton of Zürich have gained a reputation for investing extensive resources in drug areas and for going about it rather forcefully, such as making more frequent arrests" (Balvig, 1988: 88). Drug laws in Switzerland were substantially revised in 1975, when penalties were raised from a maximum of 5 years' imprisonment to 20. And for the first time "mere possession and the mere consumption of drugs, including marihuana, became explicitly punishable" (Balvig, 1988: 87).

There was a low Swiss imprisonment rate of 43.5 per 100,000 in 1972, lower than most of western Europe (Clinard, 1978: 116). Most Swiss offenders who were incarcerated (85 percent) were given sentences of six months or less (Clinard, 1978); and 69 percent of convicted offenders received suspended sentences in 1971 (Clinard, 1978: 118). Swiss prisons are very small, which may be conducive to creating prison regimes that are not harsh and do not lead to the formation of prison subcultures (Clinard, 1978: 119). In this laid-back Swiss atmosphere there were, however, some exceptions. "One-third of all the prisoners in Switzerland on any given day in 1983 were there for drug crimes" (Balvig, 1988: 91). And they are given longer sentences than other offenders, with the consequences that Swiss prisons are filled to capacity.

Iceland as a Research Site

Clinard ignored Iceland in all comparisons. We will show that patterns of law enforcement that he found in Switzerland also exist in Iceland. But we argue that Iceland might be a better candidate for analysis as a nation with little crime, having fewer serious criminal offenses than most of its European neighbors. The objective here is to study official crime rates, perceptions of crime, and control of crime in this peaceful society, which has no standing army, has not had an execution since 1830, and had a small population of approximately 272,000 people in 1998 living in an area about the size of Kentucky.

Iceland was founded around A.D. 870, and from the beginning Icelandic law emphasized equality more than other Scandinavian or Germanic countries (Nordal, 1990), but at the same time Icelanders have respected individual freedom (Finnbogason, 1971). From its beginning, Iceland has had a legislative assembly that permitted the country to be ruled democratically without a king. The hillside in southwestern Iceland where the Parliament met for many centuries in the open air is considered hallowed ground by Icelanders (Nordal, 1990: 103). From the earliest Icelandic history the rule of law was of great significance. Immigrating Icelanders brought with them Norwegian legal traditions. Miller (1990: 225) reports that there was a "rich repository of oral rules" even prior to being set down in writing and also before there was a government strong enough to enforce the law. From 930 to 1264 it is known that much of the law was recited during the meeting of the national assembly, and some contend that it was not until later that written law took precedence over oral law (Wieting and Þórlindsson, 1990).

Other evidence of the significance of law to Icelanders is found in their national literature. From their beginnings these people have placed a great importance on their origins and genealogy (Tomasson, 1980: 56). Much of this early history is found in their beloved Sagas, approximately three dozen stories (Andersson and Miller, 1989: 3) known to some extent by every Icelander. These manuscripts were written primarily during the thirteenth century about the period when the Parliament was founded, around 930 (Jochens, 1995: 171). The Sagas, in turn, are "permeated by legal lore" (Tomasson, 1980: 13). In other European countries laws had their origins in royal decrees or in the Christian religion. In kingless Iceland, however, nobility played no role in lawmaking, and Icelandic law existed well before Christianity arrived on the island. The isolation of Iceland gave it more freedom from external controls than other European nations (Miller, 1990).

It can also be noted that Iceland has a very homogeneous ethnic stock, which is virtually all white, 95 percent Lutheran, and is isolated from its nearest European neighbor by several hundred miles of ocean (see, for example, Grímsson and Broddason, 1977; Tomasson, 1980). Iceland has one of the highest standards of living in the world, even though less than one-fifth of its land surface is arable. "No other western economy is more regulated to insure full employment and none heretofore has been so successful" (Tomasson, 1980: 37). Family names are of little significance in this tiny, almost tribal island nation. A son's last name is his father's first name plus a *son* ending. A daughter's last name is also her father's first name but with a *dóttir* ending, and women retain this name after marriage. These patronymic naming practices suggest that immediate family is not so important as community. Foreigners who become Icelandic citizens are required to have Icelandic first names—to be part of the community.

With some exaggeration, Eliot Weinberger (1997) has recently described Iceland as a paradise:

> Outside the South Pacific, no ethnic group so small has its own entirely independent nation-state. . . . It is a modern Scandinavian country where everything works, and where the state protects its citizens from birth to death. There is universal education, virtually no unemployment, no poverty and no conspicuous wealth. . . . Icelanders live longer than most anywhere else. There is no pollution. . . . The use of pesticides is unknown.

Weinberger (1997) also shows that the rights of women are not forgotten:

> For the past thousand years, Icelandic women have had rights unimagined elsewhere, such as the ability to divorce and keep half the property. It was the first nation with a woman president, and is the only one with an all-woman political party with seats in Parliament.

Icelanders understandably are "vigorously patriotic and nationalistic" (Tomasson, 1980: 198). They are proud of their unique language and fiercely protect it by law from outside influences. More books are published per capita in Iceland than anywhere else in the world. Unlike many of its European neighbors, Iceland has never had an aristocracy and has never owned a colony. What, then, could be the nature of crime in such an island paradise?

The industrial revolution belatedly hit Iceland in the first decades of the twentieth century. Iceland's population has tripled since 1910, from about 85,000 then to 272,000 in 1998. In 1910 more than two-thirds of the population lived in rural areas, but in 1998 this was true of less than 10 percent of the population. During the same time, the occupational structure of Iceland changed radically. In 1910 most of the population was involved in either farming or fishing, whereas in 1998 these occupations involved only 10 percent of the population. The transformation of Icelandic society almost perfectly traces the aftermath of the European industrial revolution, only at a higher speed. Reinforced by other worldwide events, Iceland's transformation, from a backward country relying on subsistence farming and fishing into a Scandinavian-style welfare state based on industrialized fisheries, occurred in a matter of decades. After centuries of almost total isolation, Iceland increasingly came into contact with both European and North American countries. The present worldwide process of internationalization thus constitutes an even more radical departure for Iceland than for other Western countries (Gunnlaugsson and Bjarnason, 1994). As a consequence there is a mood of panic and a feeling of paradise lost.

Punishment without Crime

Despite dramatic social changes after the industrial revolution and a deepening crime concern, compared with other nations Iceland has remarkably little crime and violence. The study of the reaction to crime in this setting allows a test of the assertion that the identification and punishment of crime are necessary in all societies to maintain moral and social boundaries. With little other crime to focus on, for many years Icelandic legal authorities struggled to enforce the prohibition of beer, even while legalizing all other alcoholic beverages. Articles in the Icelandic press reflected escalating concerns with illegal drugs, even while anonymous questionnaires provided, until very recently, only a modest basis for such concerns. Correspondingly, an undercover drug police agency has been created along with a specialized drug court. Moreover, the nation's correctional system has been expanded in part to accommodate drug offenders. Compared with the prosecution of drug charges, prosecution of rape cases has been relatively difficult in Iceland, calling into question assertions of gender equality.

   Quinney's *Social Reality of Crime* (1970) noted that the nature of crime is a consequence of the definitions of the powerful, including the press, which are imposed upon a society. This is the heart of crime's social reality. In the United States police and judicial discrimination against minorities has been widely documented. For example, even when controlling for the rate of victimization, we find a positive relationship between levels of arrest for violent crime and the percentage of the population that is black, as well as between arrest rates and the amount of economic inequality in an area (Williams and Drake, 1980). And judges have been shown to discriminate against blacks in deciding on length of sentence (Farnworth and Horan, 1980). On the other hand, studies of Iceland found little evidence of social class divisions (Tomasson, 1980: 51), nor has crime been found to be a serious social problem (Ólafsdóttir, 1985). In addition to never having had a nobility, unlike most other European nations, Iceland provides all education and medical care virtually free of charge, further reducing social class disparities. Given this commitment to public education it should not be surprising that Iceland has a well-educated populace with nearly 100 percent literacy, as well as more books published per capita than any other nation. The question is, What is the social reality of crime among these well-informed people who experience no great concentrations of wealth and power?

It is important to keep in mind that Durkheim (1964) argued that some crime is necessary in any society, irrespective of the local stratification system. Especially during periods of instability and social change, crime and its punishment help maintain the moral boundaries of a group and thus increase social solidarity. The experience of a Roman Catholic seminarian may shed some light on this issue. In his experience masturbation was likely to be the most serious offense in a seminary, convent, or monastery. Every morning in the seminary where he trained, there was a long line of seminarians awaiting confession, and everyone knew what they were confessing. Masturbation was condemned in the strongest possible terms by the leaders of the seminary as the moral equivalent of murder. This illustrates the general point that no matter what the nature of the most serious offense in any given social situation, it is likely to be considered a profound offense by the local authorities.

Erikson's (1966) research on the origins of the proscription of witchcraft in the Massachusetts Bay Colony is especially relevant in this regard. Even though this research deals with a society that existed over 300 years ago, it still provides a parallel to modern Iceland. Erikson (1966) found that the Massachusetts Bay Colony was an island of civilization in the midst of a massive wilderness, just as Iceland is an island in the midst of the frigid North Atlantic. Erikson argued that witch hunting started in the colony because of rapid social change in the community, due to both internal power shifts and outside threats. He argued that this crisis of witches was actually created by the community in an effort to restore moral order in this transient period by punishing certain people and behavior not believed to be in tune with rudimentary community standards. Through these punishments, the group publicly affirmed its moral boundaries and thus was able to strengthen its collective identity and cohesion by openly asserting that certain acts would not be tolerated.

Erikson (1966), moreover, argues that although geographical location is significant, it alone does not determine the conditions of boundary maintenance, for collective identity plays a critical role. The people of a community spend most of their lives in close contact with one another, sharing a common sphere of experience, which makes them feel that they belong to a special "kind" and live in a special "place" (Erikson, 1966: 9). Similarly, according to Christie (1993: 27), Iceland is seen as "a country beyond the reach of many influences, and has such a small population that 'most people' know each other,—and maybe even need each other. Honour may still count." This is precisely what Icelanders are afraid of losing and explains their deepening concern about crime.

The Linkage of Crime to Social Stratification

Chambliss offers a contrasting point of view in noting that events such as cited by Erikson are not inconsistent with other interpretations, including the observation that societal leaders in the Massachusetts Bay Colony sought to dominate local citizens through punishments (Chambliss, 1973). The social context was such that punishment of witches may well have served to increase solidarity within the group, but Chambliss noted that nonetheless the personal interests served were clearly those of the leaders of the group. Later Chambliss recognized (1979: 5) that "one is hard pressed to find examples of modern social scientists defending the pure forms of either of these models. Everyone, it seems, recognizes that there is some truth in both claims."

In addition to its low rates of serious offenses, Iceland's total lack of marked poverty and its relative lack of social and economic stratification (Gunnlaugsson and Galliher, 1986) make it a good candidate for our analysis to assess the claims of conflict theory regarding the relationship between crime control and social stratification. While all social classes are found in Iceland, the differences between these classes have been less pronounced than in many other industrialized democracies (*Vísbending*, 1994). As Tomasson (1980: 195) has noted: "There are few things Icelanders believe more about themselves than that theirs is a country where there is equality among interacting individuals and equality of opportunity." Correspondingly, Iceland has one of the highest standards of living in the world, with an unemployment rate hovering around 1 percent (Tomasson, 1980: 36), even though unemployment increased during the early 1990s. Given Iceland's special history, lack of marked social stratification, and corresponding collective identity conceptions, one would expect few crime problems to emerge. And on the basis of the experiences in other egalitarian societies, one would predict only the most rudimentary development of this nation's criminal justice system (Schwartz, 1954). Yet in spite of still having relatively low crime rates, the criminal justice system in Iceland has in recent decades grown and become more professionalized.

In view of such findings the question becomes, What are the origins and operation of law enforcement in a country such as Iceland, where social, racial, and economic stratification has not been found to be as pervasive as in such other nations as the United States or the United Kingdom? Assuming that there has traditionally been relatively little social and economic stratification, it also seems predictable that Iceland would have experienced relatively little crime compared with societies with more pronounced economic differences and racial heterogeneity.

Searching for Nations with Little Need for Boundary Maintenance

Erikson (1966) found that as the Massachusetts Bay Colony became less and less isolated from the outside world and with "realignment of power within the group" (Erikson, 1966: 68), artificial means of boundary maintenance became more essential. The means of boundary maintenance involved the location and punishment of witches.

> Massachusetts had been founded as a lonely pocket of civilization in the midst of a howling wilderness. . . . [Later on] the settlers had lost sight of their local frontiers. . . . The original settlers had landed in a wilderness full of "wild beasts and wilder men"; yet sixty years later, sitting many miles from the nearest frontier in the prosperous seaboard town of Boston . . . [after] the visible traces of that wilderness had receded out of sight, the settlers invented a new one by finding the shapes of the forest in the middle of the community itself. (Erikson, 1966: 157)

Thus, the witchcraft craze was born. Our task is to locate a modern nation that is isolated from its neighbors, much as was originally true of the Massachusetts Bay Colony. Again, Iceland appears to be a good candidate, since it is separated by several hundred miles of the North Atlantic from its nearest European neighbor.

Crime in Scandinavia and the Neglect of Iceland

Over the past 30 years, myriad studies have verified relatively low levels of crime in the Nordic region. Some research has drawn on surveys of criminal victimization and fear of crime (Kutschinsky, 1968; Brun-Gulbrandsen, 1971; Aromaa, 1974, 1990; Hauge and Wolf, 1974;

Balvig, 1990). Other research has dealt with press reports of crime (Hauge, 1965). Still other studies have relied on official reports, including records of prison populations (Lenke, 1980), levels of violence (von Hofer, 1990), and international comparisons of arrest rates across countries (Wolf, 1971). All have ignored Iceland as well as the Faeroe Islands.

Iceland seems to have been almost totally ignored by students of crime and punishment and, surprisingly, even by Nordic social scientists, perhaps because it is small and remote. A recent study of trends in crime and criminal punishment in Nordic countries made no mention of Iceland (Joutsen, 1992) but reported a decreasing use of imprisonment in the other four Nordic nations, as well as the use of shorter sentences. These patterns are perhaps best illustrated by Finland, where between 1950 and 1985 the median sentence dropped from 7.6 months to 3.3 months (Joutsen, 1992). One writer mentioned as an aside that the legal framework in Iceland is similar to Denmark's (Andenaes, 1968), and another intentionally excluded Iceland because of its small population (Lenke, 1980). Why Iceland has been ignored can be at least partly inferred from a recent book by Christie (1993). He noted that Iceland in 1990 had only 41 prisoners for every 100,000 of its people, which put it below almost all other nations of the world and certainly below its western European neighbors (Christie, 1993: 28). Perhaps another reason no mention is made of Iceland is that, unlike other Nordic nations, Iceland has systematically collected few records of crime that could facilitate international comparisons, as we will demonstrate.

Adler (1983) has found that the best predictor of crime rates across nations is the amount of population growth per annum. Low-crime nations typically "have lower than average population density, lower than average urban population density, [and] lower than average urban populations" (Adler, 1983: 10). However, Adler ignores Iceland, even though it has both a small and a homogeneous population in addition to a relatively low population density. The last factor makes a nation such as Iceland especially interesting, since many behavioral scientists see population density as a triggering mechanism for aggression and violence (Gaylord and Galliher, 1991).

Icelandic Crime and Delinquency: International Comparisons

Weinberger (1997), whose idyllic descriptions of Iceland we saw in an earlier section, continues his mythmaking about Iceland: "It is nonviolent: no army, few handguns, little crime; . . . small children walk in the city alone"—exactly what Icelanders are afraid that they are losing. Icelandic conviction records were published for 1946–1952 and for 1966–

1977, the latter period being when the last court report appeared. During these periods crimes against property increased, whereas violent crimes did not (Ólafsdóttir, 1985). Another scholar (van den Hoonaard, 1991) evaluating the same data also found Icelandic crime increasing, although Reykjavík's share decreased. Other research in Iceland indicates 47 murders during 1900–1979, with two-thirds of the offenders having psychiatric disorders (Pétursson and Guðjónsson, 1981; Guðjónsson and Pétursson, 1984). Archer and Gartner (1984) collected Icelandic crime conviction data as part of a comparative study of 111 countries. They were able to secure Icelandic crime data for 1969 through 1971. During this three-year period they found 3 murder convictions, 6 for manslaughter, 14 assaults, 5 rapes, 244 thefts, and no robberies, at a time when the population increased from 200,000 to 210,000 (Archer and Gartner, 1984: 173ff.). By comparison they found that for the same years in Switzerland, approximately six times as much serious crime per capita was reported. For Denmark the murder rate was approximately twice as high, and for all other crimes even higher. For Sweden the murder rate was approximately five times as high, and again much higher for all other crimes. All this suggests that if one were to use the official record to isolate a country with little crime, Iceland rather than Switzerland would seem to be the ideal candidate.

During the 1980s several studies dealing with crime in Iceland appeared, reflecting both an increased concern with crime in the nation and an increased professionalism in crime analysis. These studies dealt with everything from drug use to homicide and used government records of incarceration and the scant conviction records (arrest records have not been systematically kept), as well as anonymous questionnaires. Also, a cross-national survey of public attitudes toward the police and crime was conducted (Baldursson, 1981a, b). During 1970–1989, a total of 24 cases of murder were recorded (Harðardóttir, 1991: 50; see also Guðjónsson and Pétursson, 1990). Kristmundsson (1989: 12, 20, 26) found increases also in the conviction and incarceration of property offenders, drug offenders, and those guilty of driving while intoxicated (DWIs) during that same period. Moreover, Kristmundsson (1985: 71) had earlier found that 24 percent of Icelanders aged 16 to 36 admitted they had used cannabis at least once (the term *cannabis* is used in this volume to indicate either marihuana or hashish or a combination of the two).

In 1989 a government committee issued a report on sex crimes in Iceland, where it was found that on the average between 1977 and 1983 approximately 20 cases of rape were reported annually to the State Criminal Investigative Police (Rape Report, 1989: 137). This was not believed to be markedly different from other Nordic countries. Yet, according to 1993

Table 1.1. Crimes known to the police in Nordic capitals in 1993 (rates per 100,000 inhabitants)

	Homicide	Forcible rape	Aggravated assault	Narcotics	Robbery
Reykjavík	0.9	10.0	3.4	163	29.3
Copenhagen	2.8	15.0	283.1	2,196	331.2
Oslo	2.5	17.5	67.6	735	214.2
Stockholm	5.5	28.7	53.0	655	268.0
Helsinki	2.2	13.2	41.6	230	169.0

Sources: Interpol, 1993; and records provided by the Reykjavík police.

Interpol records of crimes known to the police (see table 1.1), the rate of rape was lower in Reykjavík than in other Nordic capitals. Research dealing with less serious offenses such as shoplifting (Guðjónsson, 1982b) and juvenile delinquency (Guðjónsson, 1982a) also paints a picture of a relatively crime-free environment in Iceland.

Although well-known problems exist in international crime comparisons, it bears noting that table 1.1 indicates that Reykjavík remains lower than other Nordic capitals for all serious forms of crime. In addition, per capita imprisonment rates show Iceland below almost all other European nations (table 1.2). Yet the overall impression of Iceland, which we will discuss in chapter 2, is that of a society which has experienced some increase in the level of crime in recent decades, associated with a deepening concern about crime, especially drug offenses, drunk driving, and violent crimes. In comparative perspective though, the crime rate for offenses such as homicide or for other crimes, including rape and robbery, has continued to be markedly lower than that of neighboring countries. Yet one is handicapped in any long-term comparative analysis by the absence of any systematic annual records of crime published by the Icelandic police or courts through most of this century. This shows the low priority of such events compared with fishing and weather reports, for which high-quality records have routinely been collected and published.

However, demonstrating a continuing concern with the problems of the young in recent years, considerable attention has been given to youth and violence, as well as to youth and drugs. In a study of 15- and 16-year-old Icelanders, Bjarnason and Sigurðardóttir (1995) concluded that being a victim of violent crime is positively associated with commission of violent acts, as well as with alcohol and drug use. A more recent study of violent behavior among 10th graders, based on self-report questionnaires, found positive associations between violence and family breakdown, type of peer group associations, and life-style, including smoking

Table 1.2. Prison figures for selected European countries in 1993 (numbers and rates per 100,000 inhabitants)

	Rate	Number		Rate	Number
Northern Ireland	118	1,902	Belgium	72	7,203
Scotland	115	5,900	Denmark	71	3,702
Spain	115	45,711	Greece	68	6,524
Portugal	111	10,904	Sweden	66	5,794
Luxembourg	107	425	Finland	62	3,132
United Kingdom	92	53,435	Norway	60	2,607
Austria	91	7,099	Ireland	60	2,108
England & Wales	89	45,633	Turkey	52	31,304
Italy	89	50,794	Holland	51	7,843
France	86	51,134	Iceland	39	103
Germany	81	65,838	Cyprus	30	188
Switzerland	81	5,627			

Source: Michael Cavadino and James Dignan, The Penal System: An Introduction, 2d ed. (London: Sage Publications, 1997), p. 13; reprinted by permission of Sage Publications Ltd.

and drinking, poor school performance, and delinquent behavior (Þórlindsson and Bernburg, 1996).

An earlier survey of 13- to 16-year-old Icelanders (Skinner, 1986: 287) found very little drug use, with over 92 percent reporting they had never used any illegal drug, and this study reported no evidence of a local "drug culture." A study conducted in 1994 found that slightly fewer than 20 percent of students who were 16 to 20 years old had used cannabis at least once, and fewer than 5 percent had used the drug more than 10 times (Kaldalóns et al., 1994: 7). This is not markedly different from other Nordic countries, the rates being somewhat higher than those of youth in Norway but lower than those of Denmark. Proportionately, in 1995 more 10th graders in Iceland admitted that they had used cannabis (10 percent) than 10th graders in Norway and Sweden (6 percent) and in Finland (5 percent), but fewer in Iceland than in the Faeroe Islands (11 percent) and in Denmark, which topped out at 17 percent (Hibell et al., 1997: 103). Research such as this has fueled the concern about drugs in Iceland. Hibell and his colleagues' survey of 26 European countries found that overall the average use of marihuana or hashish was 12 percent, which was higher than the use in Nordic countries alone (Hibell et al., 1997: 103). Even more recent research indicates that life-time prevalence of cannabis use in Iceland is 18.6 percent, again higher than that found in other Nordic countries, except Denmark, at 30.1 percent. However, the figure for those admitting use in the past six months was much lower; at 1.6 percent Iceland was similar to other Nordic nations (Gunnlaugsson, 1998: 283). Thus, it appears that for the most part drug use consists of experimentation and recreational use of cannabis among younger age groups, who often quit with increasing age (Gunnlaugsson, 1998).

Reflective of Icelanders' collective identity and long-term concern with substance abuse, this small nation maintained a highly unusual beer prohibition for over 70 years, until 1989. This law was justified as a means of protecting the nation's youth (Gunnlaugsson and Galliher, 1986). As we will show, it was repeatedly argued in Parliament and elsewhere that beer was a steppingstone drug invariably leading to hard liquor, which curiously was legal. This concern with alcohol in turn was traditionally based on beliefs about Icelanders' special vulnerability due to their Icelandic heritage. For example, one member of Parliament (MP) noted: "Icelanders are not able to use alcohol as civilized persons, their nature is still too much of the Viking kind, they get too excited and brutal" (Gunnlaugsson and Galliher, 1986: 341). And public opinion is obviously important in Iceland, as reflected in the frequent use of surveys. Surveys on the issue of beer prohibition were repeatedly conducted, and until the 1980s most Icelanders supported this prohibition. There continues to be wide agreement that teenage drinking is a problem (Roberts and Krakauer, 1990).

Research Plan

Ultimately, to dismiss the impact of crime rates on patterns of punishment, it might be most convincing to search for nations with little crime. To minimize the impact of social structure on criminal punishment, we might begin with a search for nations with relatively little social stratification. In addition, the need to control for social structure also requires a search for nations with the least need for artificial attempts to increase their collective conscience or boundary maintenance. Presumably homogeneous nations experiencing little crime and possessing the most clearly defined natural geographical boundaries would be ideal choices. It is our contention that Iceland is a good candidate, for it appears to satisfy all these conditions.

Methods

This study of crime in Iceland utilizes both quantitative and qualitative data to assess public perceptions of crime and experience with crime. We use official records, newspaper accounts, survey data, and records of parliamentary debate. This study draws on official documents such as police, court, and prison records, as well as interviews with prison directors, guards, and inmates and both past and present governmental officials to supplement scanty official records. A review of every issue of the major daily newspaper, the *Morgunblaðið*, was conducted for particular years between 1969 and 1993, spaced at four- or five-year intervals and chosen intentionally in order to highlight particular controversies. Such a review allows an analysis of the frequency of crime-related news accounts, and the nature of these reports thus provides an understanding of how crime is perceived by both the media and the general public. Comprehensive public surveys of attitudes were conducted in 1989 and in 1994 to provide another more direct measure of public perceptions of crime in Iceland. These surveys addressed questions regarding the extent to which Icelanders were concerned about crime in general and about crimes of different types, the extent to which they felt safe from crime in their communities, and whether they had been the victims of crime. The records of debate in Iceland's parliament were drawn on in the cases of both sex crimes and drug offenses that had sparked major legislative debates. Everything quoted from any of these sources or from any of the other Icelandic sources listed in the references was translated by Helgi Gunnlaugsson.

Theoretical Focus

The chapters that follow attempt to locate the social reality of crime in Iceland, first by assembling in chapter 2 existing official records of crime over the past century. Scanty historical records indicate little interest in crime, at least until very recently. In chapter 3 we will discuss Iceland's long tradition of beer prohibition, which was eventually repealed in 1989 as a consequence of increased contacts abroad where beer is widely accepted. Recently increasing newspaper accounts of crime are analyzed in chapter 4. It has been documented that through the mass media most citizens experience and understand crime and, moreover, that these public perceptions are often unrelated to the crime actually occurring in the community (Davis, 1952). Chapter 5 reports on another dimension of the social reality of crime in Iceland: recent surveys of citizen perceptions of crime and experiences with crime, reflecting increasing concerns. This type of information is indispensable in measuring the impact of news reports, official records, and direct victimization upon public opinion. The nation's uneven law enforcement against sex crimes is explored in chapter 6 and contrasted with other increasingly stringent enforcement practices. Chapter 7 emphasizes how the legal system has been distorted by procedures put in place to fight drug offenses through the creation of a specialized drug police force and a drug court. The history and recent growth and bureaucratization of the police and the courts are explored in chapter 8. The growth of the Icelandic prison system as a response to the increasing crime concern is described in chapter 9. Chapter 10 demonstrates how a functionalist theory involving boundary maintenance can be used to inform the nature of crime and crime control in Iceland. In recent years Icelanders increasingly have come into contact with the outside world, broken their long-term isolation, and experienced rapid social transformation, becoming more like other nations. This change has in turn resulted in the repeal of beer prohibition, which was replaced by a war on drugs as the primary means of boundary maintenance.

2

Scant Records of Little Crime
Official Icelandic Crime Reports, 1881–1996

The reasons for the relative absence of criminological studies in Iceland are at least twofold. The first is that the social sciences in Iceland, including criminology, date back only to the 1970s. Another likely explanation, as noted in chapter 1, is that crime statistics have not been easily accessible because of irregular or nonexistent record keeping by local authorities, making criminological research difficult or impossible. What have been available in crime statistics are occasionally published reports of legal outcomes of the criminal courts for brief time periods. These reports were, however, not issued for the time periods 1926–1945 or 1953–1965 and have not been published since 1977. Records of crimes known to the police were not easily available until 1989; in addition, the Office of Public Prosecutions has kept statistics of arraigned persons for only the last few years, and these are not published. Consequently, it has been difficult to obtain a detailed historical picture of crime in Iceland. The United States, by contrast, devotes considerable resources to annual compilation of crime statistics of all kinds. Records of arrests, trials, fines, property seizures, imprisonment, and executions are routinely collected, published, and distributed. For American law enforcement it is unthinkable that any government agency would allow a lapse in official record keeping.

In this brief chapter we review the official reality of crime in Iceland dating back to the nineteenth century. First we review available court statistics, followed by recent statistics on indictments, and finally we present information on "special penal code" violations, which primarily involve alcohol-related offenses. Institutional records indicate that during the early twentieth century a large proportion of those sentenced to jail had been convicted of some type of alcohol-related offense, reflecting the perceived seriousness of substance abuse.

Clinard (1978) has noted that in Switzerland the only crime data collected on the national level were for convictions, even though such

18

information is widely recognized as unrepresentative of the crime actually occurring in the community. In part the explanation is that "there has been no urgency for the national government to gather these data, because crime has not been considered a major national problem" (Clinard, 1978: 34). If only scant information is available in Switzerland, the situation is even worse in Iceland. Yet, despite this state of affairs, analysis of the meager information available should at least help give some insight into the problem of crime in Iceland over time; it should reveal the type of offenses most common in the criminal courts, as well as the legal response to those offenses. We must emphasize that this is not exhaustive information of crime trends but is merely suggestive at best.

It remains an open question as to why local authorities have not been more efficient in both the keeping and the publication of crime records. One explanation may have to do with the nature of the bureaucracy itself. It may sound plausible to say that in this tiny nation there has not been the institutional capacity to meet the needs of modern record keeping. But as noted earlier, record keeping in other fields has been more thorough, such as for the population census, for the housing and construction industry, and for the fishing industry. Another, and perhaps more likely explanation, has to do with authorities' perceptions of the crime problem. This lack of public information on crime may well be due to the possibility that crime (just as in Switzerland) has not been perceived as a serious social problem, and thus thorough record keeping has not been a high priority. It could be argued that if crime was perceived to be a serious social problem, a statistical account of its content and volume would have been required by the governing body. This has not been the case until very recently and has therefore resulted in crime records that are primitive compared with those of most industrial nations. It could be expected, however, that as more systematic records of crime are maintained, the level of citizen concern will increase as well. Citizens no longer will have to guess about the dimensions of the crime problem in Iceland.

Early Court Records

Records of conviction and prosecution for the 45-year period 1881–1925 indicate that in Iceland property crimes such as burglary, vandalism, and theft predominated, totaling more than three-quarters of all offenses (see "property crimes," top panel of table 2.1). No murders were recorded during this stretch. On the basis of these reports, it appears that abortion was perceived as being as significant as manslaughter, since it was included in the same category. Rape was not separated from other sex offenses and provides an example of the difficulties in the use of these early court statis-

Table 2.1. Early criminal court convictions, by type of offense, 1881–1925 and 1946–1952

	Number	Percent	Mean per year
	1881–1925		
Murder	0	0	0
Manslaughter and abortion	20	2	0.4
Sex crimes	74	6	1.6
Other violence	85	7	1.8
Property crimes	992	78	22
Other	94	7	2
Totals	1,265	100	27.8
	1946–1952		
Murder	1	1	0.1
Manslaughter	53	3	7.6
Rape	6	1	0.8
Other sex crimes	23	2	3.3
Other assaults	380	27	54.3
Property crimes	785	57	112.1
Other	125	9	17.8
Totals	1,373	100	196.0

Source: Justice Statistics: 1881–1925 (1930); 1946–1952 (1958).

tics. In total, there was an average (or mean) of 28 convictions per year and an average of approximately only 4 convictions per year for violent crime. In 1910 the nation's population stood at just over 85,000. The annual mean conviction rate for each decade from 1881 to 1925 varied between 0.31 and 0.63 per 100,000 for those older than 14 and between 0.22 and 0.43 for the entire population.

The court reports for 1946–1952 (bottom panel of table 2.1) were more precise in their categorization of crimes. Now rape was separated from other sex offenses, and abortion was no longer included with manslaughter. Convictions increased significantly, with slightly more offenses occurring during this 7-year period than in the entire 45-year period of 1881–1925. Between the turn of the century and 1950, the population of Iceland had almost doubled to nearly 144,000. Overall the average number of crimes per year increased sevenfold from the earlier period to the later one. In addition there was a whopping 17-fold increase in violent crime. The conviction rate during this period was 1.30 per 100,000 for those older than 14—more than double the 1881–1925 rate. For the entire population, the rate was 0.89. However, whether this increase adequately represents crime in society is still an open question. Here we have only court convictions, not all crimes known to police. This increase might also suggest more efficient legal processing of criminal cases and better record keeping by public officials.

Modern Court Records

On the heels of these increases immediately after World War II, an additional increase in convictions appeared for all types of crimes from 1966 to 1977 (see table 2.2). This was especially true for rape and murder. According to the court reports, murder for the first time became at least an annual event in Iceland. By 1970 the nation's population stood at approximately 204,000, and conviction rates per 100,000 inhabitants during 1966–1977 varied annually between 0.3 and 1.1 for sex crimes, 7.5 and 11.4 for other violence, and 34.1 to 44.4 for property offenses. Records of court convictions have not been published since the reports were done for the period from 1966 to 1977.

Records of indictments for 1978–1985 and 1989–1994, although never published, were provided by the director of prosecutions (table 2.3). Indictments suggest that overall the mean number of crimes per year approximately doubled between the period 1966–1977 and these later periods. Yet, indictments are not identical to court convictions, which previous statistics are based on. Indictment rates varied annually between 182.0 and 304.0 per 100,000.

According to table 2.3, indictments increased between the two time periods, from an average of about 410 a year in 1978–1985 to nearly 483 a year during 1989–1994. As for crime categories, sex crimes, other

Table 2.2. Modern criminal court convictions, by type of offense, 1966–1977

	Number	Percent	Mean per year
Murder	20	1	1.7
Manslaughter	100	3	8.3
Rape	24	1	2.0
Other sex crimes	44	1	3.7
Other assaults	275	8	22.9
Property crimes	2,992	85	249.3
Other	45	1	3.8
Totals	3,500	100	291.7

Source: Justice Statistics: 1966–1968 (1973); 1969–1971 (1975); 1972–1974 (1978); 1975–1977 (1983).

Table 2.3. Persons indicted and arraigned, by type of offense, 1978–1985 and 1989–1994

	Number	Percent	Mean per year	Rate per 100,000 for entire period
		1978–1985		
Murder	12	0.3	1.5	0.6
Manslaughter	6	0.1	0.7	0.4
Rape	68	1.6	8.5	3.3
Other sex crimes	64	1.5	8.0	2.8
Other assaults	481	11.0	60.1	25.0
Traffic offenses[a]	451	10.3	56.4	23.5
Property crimes	3,281	75.2	410.1	171.0
Totals	4,363	100	545.3	226.6
		1989–1994		
Murder	10	0.2	1.6	0.6
Attempted homicide	6	0.1	1.0	0.4
Robbery	27	0.6	4.5	0.16
Sex crimes	167	4.0	27.8	10.7
Other assaults	677	16.1	112.8	43.4
Traffic offenses	253	6.0	42.1	16.2
Property crimes	2,897	68.9	482.8	185.7
Other	174	4.1	29.0	11.2
Totals	4,184	100	701.6	268.36

Source: Records provided by the director of prosecutions.
[a]Information available only for 1981–1985.

assaults, and property crimes increased the most. Property crimes increased in excess of 70 per year, while sex crimes and other assaults nearly doubled. However, if we control for population, the increase is more modest between the two time periods, as seen by the rates shown in table 2.3.

Violations of the special penal laws are not included in total indictments and convictions. These offenses primarily involve violations of alcohol and drug statutes. Criminal court cases involving drunk driving and smuggling accounted for a third of all criminal court cases for the period 1966–1971 (Tomasson, 1980: 189). In Iceland the high rate of traffic offenses involving alcohol is consistent with other Nordic countries. In addition, in Iceland between 1929 and 1938 over half of the prison population served time for alcohol offenses such as illegal brewing (Heiðdal, 1957:

160). Of the 673 prisoners during this period, 345 were found guilty of alcohol-related offenses.

All told 75.8 percent of those convicted of violating these laws (during 1978–1987) were found guilty of drunk driving; another 16.1 percent, of violating the narcotics provisions. Together they make up 91.9 percent of the total of 1,836 such convictions (traffic = 1,392 and narcotics = 296). Between 1974 and 1990 an annual average of 2,459 were arrested for driving while intoxicated (Traffic Council, 1991). This annual figure represents approximately 1 percent of the nation's population. Those arrested a third time have faced a mandatory prison sentence. Correspondingly, in recent years prison figures indicate that the number of inmates serving sentences for DWI routinely surpassed one-fifth of the entire prison population (Prison and Probation Administration, annual report, 1995).

Contemporary Police Records

Records of the State Criminal Investigative Police (SCIP) investigations were published annually between 1991 (which included data back through 1988) and 1994, and since then crime frequencies have still been available upon request. This agency was responsible for all major criminal cases in the Reykjavík area, where the majority of Icelanders live. In addition, this agency was occasionally asked to investigate major cases elsewhere in the rural areas of the country. Therefore the SCIP records should provide an adequate representation of crimes known to the police. In 1997 a new state police unit was established to replace SCIP functions and to serve as a centralized force, with data gathered nationally.

Table 2.4 indicates that there have been some crime changes in recent years. Though fluctuating, the total number of cases has tended to increase, but burglaries have shown a dramatic increase, whereas property crimes other than burglary and theft seem to have decreased. According to the SCIP report for 1993, burglaries and thefts consisted in large part of taking items such as radios and CD players from automobiles. In 1993 there were 1,010 such cases compared to 344 cases of residential burglary. Property crimes such as fraud, forgery, and bad checks seem to be on a downward trend. This might suggest blocked opportunities for such crime because financial transactions in the society have become increasingly computerized. For example, credit and debit cards can be routinely scanned electronically prior to each use. Burglaries, by comparison, have increased, with opportunities for them most likely perceived as comparatively easy. The SCIP report for 1993 stated:

Table 2.4. Number of cases investigated by the State Criminal Investigative Police, by type of offense, 1988–1996

	1988	1989	1990	1991	1992	1993	1994	1995	1996
Burglary	1,298	1,575	1,575	1,468	1,837	1,873	2,208	2,415	2,236
Theft	1,198	1,553	1,418	1,219	1,337	1,423	1,479	1,456	—
Other property crimes[a]	—	3,165	2,569	2,412	3,420	2,382	1,240	1,258	424
Rape	31	18	15	17	17	25	26	19	20
Attempted rape	—	2	6	3	4	3	10	6	—
Other sex offenses	66	59	62	71	65	69	83	84	55
Homicide	6	0	1	3	2	1	0	0	0
Attempted homicide	—	2	0	2	5	1	0	1	1
Other violence	133	125	101	98	90	91	90	93	105

Source: SCIP, annual reports, 1991–1994 (1991 report contains data for 1988–1990); SCIP printouts for 1994–1996.
Note: Drug and traffic offenses are not investigated by the SCIP.
[a]Including fraud, check fraud, and forgery. Here violations and not cases are recorded.

It has not been studied but is evident to most of those who become involved in handling these cases that a group of relatively few people are
responsible for most of these crimes. . . . Police officers know that a
great many of these offenders are either alcoholics, or drug addicts, or
both. If they are not cured of their illness they will continue their criminal activities despite prison sentences. (SCIP, annual report, 1994: 17)

The focus on individual problems rather than on social structure corresponds, as we will show later, with the survey data as well as with news
reports.

Contemporary Prison Statistics

Prior to 1989 the Justice Ministry directed the nation's prison system. In
1989 a new independent agency, the Prison and Probation Administration,
was established to direct the placement of convicted criminals in Iceland's
various prisons. This agency receives those convicted in the nation's courts
and is charged with ensuring that prisoners receive treatment, including
mental health services (law no. 48, 1988). In 1995 the agency had a staff of
10, including a criminologist. They determine the appropriate institution
for each of those sentenced to prison and assist in determining suitability
for parole. Table 2.5 shows the annual number of those under the supervi-
sion of this agency from 1989 to 1996, by type of sentence, and indicates
some changes in recent years, especially increases in the number of those
receiving a fine. Because the national prison system in recent years was
generally operating at capacity, allowing no spurts in incarceration, more
convictions resulted in criminal fines, which, of course, are not constrained

Table 2.5. Court records of the number sentenced to the Prison and Probation
Administration, by type of sentence, 1989–1996

	1989	1990	1991	1992	1993	1994	1995	1996
Incarceration	378	343	417	317	357	449	378	360
Probation	332	383	593	385	388	421	373	366
Fine	252	224	284	232	277	451	554	483
Totals	962	950	1,294	934	1,022	1,321	1,305	1,209

Source: Prison and Probation Administration, annual reports, 1989–1996
(data for 1985–1988 contained in 1989 report).
Note: A combination of sentences is possible for each conviction. Thus, the
numbers of incarcerations shown in these years do not match the numbers shown
for the same years in table 2.6 because those data refer to people imprisoned each
year. In contrast, the data in this table refer to the total number of persons
sentenced in each year.

Table 2.6. Percentage distribution of incarcerations in Icelandic prisons, by type of crime committed, 1985–1997

	1985	1986	1987	1988	1989	1990	1991	1992	1993	1994	1995	1996	1997
Homicide	5	4	4	4	4	5	4	4	5	4	2	1	2
Property crimes	55	53	52	50	54	49	48	49	50	47	43	48	44
Traffic violations	21	22	23	19	25	29	29	24	20	19	22	17	12
Drug violations	7	11	10	11	7	7	6	8	8	11	14	13	18
Sex crimes	4	2	2	4	4	6	6	5	9	7	7	8	8
Other violence	7	5	7	8	4	2	5	6	4	7	6	7	11
Other	1	3	2	4	2	2	2	4	4	5	6	6	5
Total number	244	296	282	284	334	342	343	334	305	317	368	417	311

Source: Prison and Probation Administration, annual reports, 1989–1996 (data for 1985–1988 contained in 1989 report).

by institutional size. However, most recently, prison facilities have been modernized, and more prison space has been created.

Institutional records of prisoners for 1985–1996 reflect an emphasis on confining those convicted of property, traffic, and drug offenses, in descending order (as shown in table 2.6). Property offenders varied from 43 percent to 55 percent of the prison population, while traffic violators accounted for 12 to 29 percent, and those involved with drugs, 5 to 14 percent of prisoners. Table 2.6 shows a gradual increase in all three categories from the mid-1980s to the 1990s. The national prison population was approximately 28 per 100,000 in 1980 (Prison Committee Report, 1992: 56) and increased to 38 per 100,000 in 1993 (Prison and Probation Administration, annual report for 1993–1994: 21), but lowered to 35 per 100,000 by the end of 1998, mostly because of new alternatives to prison.

In late 1995, a new prison building was completed, which increased the existing national prison system capacity above the previous level of about 100. Table 2.6 clearly shows the increasing prison population, from a total of 244 incarcerations in 1985 to 417 in 1996. The construction program was also initiated to close some aging prison facilities and to renovate others.

In addition to these prison population figures, from 1985 to 1994 between 60 percent and 68 percent of those incarcerated in the Reykjavík city jail were there for public intoxication (ranging from 3,369 in 1989 to 4,594 in 1987), according to the Reykjavík police records. Thus, in a city of only about 100,000 citizens the police have arrested several thousand for public drunkenness every year. Half of the jail capacity in Reykjavík has been used for public drunkenness. Therefore, it is apparent that much police effort is directed against public intoxication. This suggests that alcohol-related offenses are considered a serious social problem in Iceland, as Ólafsdóttir and Helgason (1988) have shown. Even so, official accounts of alcohol consumption per capita show Icelanders consume markedly less than people in most other Western nations (Swedish Council for Information on Alcohol and Other Drugs, 1993). A popular explanation for this apparent inconsistency has been that Icelanders are binge drinkers.

Increasing Crime Recording and Increasing Crime

This brief chapter demonstrates a long-term, half-hearted effort in Iceland to maintain official criminal justice records. Unlike other nations of the industrialized West, Iceland until the last decade compiled only sketchy information on police, court, and prison activities. According to these admittedly scanty records, there has been a slow but constant increase of crime in the last few decades. These reports, though scattered, include conclusive evidence that substance abuse is a dominant, long-term theme in Icelandic law enforcement, as reflected in rates of DWIs, drug violations, and public drunkenness. This will be born out in later chapters describing this nation's history of beer prohibition and its drug police. Increased crime reporting and escalating fear of crime are mutually reinforcing, and both contribute to a growing sense of loss of control and loss of collective identity.

3
Prohibition of Beer in Iceland

Understanding Icelandic Beer Prohibition through American Eyes

In a study of the Woman's Christian Temperance Union (WCTU), Gusfield (1963) observed that in the early 1900s national prohibition of alcohol in the United States was largely the result of the efforts of middle-class, rural Protestants who felt they were losing their position of dominance in American society. As America was becoming more urban, more Catholic, and more secular, the prohibition law "established the victory of Protestant over Catholic, rural over urban, tradition over modernity, the middle class over both the lower and upper strata" (Gusfield, 1963: 7). Total abstinence was seen by the rural Protestants as the solution to lower-class poverty, so common, for example, among the urban European Catholic immigrants in the early 1900s. Much of the motivation claimed by those supporting Prohibition was an "attempt to alleviate suffering through humanitarian actions by those in advantageous positions or to reform the habits of the suffering as a way to the improvement of both their character and their material situation" (Gusfield, 1955: 223). The significance of Prohibition was that "it marked the public affirmation of the abstemious, ascetic qualities of American Protestantism" (Gusfield, 1963: 8). Gusfield (1963) observed that status politics typically involves a struggle over symbols to secure deference whereas class politics is usually characterized by a conflict over material issues.

Even though the prohibition law in America was widely violated and only grudgingly and selectively enforced, its mere existence demonstrated the superiority of the rural Protestant way of life. Symbolic legislation does not depend upon law enforcement for its effect, unlike what Gusfield (1967) calls instrumental legislation, which actually attempts to control human behavior. Signs of symbolic legislation are found when there is a law that is obviously unenforced and even unenforceable or that appears on its face to make no real difference in the lives of those it is supposed to benefit.

29

However, in both the United States and the United Kingdom there is some evidence that allegedly symbolic legislation also has instrumental qualities. For example, in the case of America's alcohol prohibition, some of the law's middle-class supporters hoped that it would serve the instrumental purpose of controlling worker behavior (Timberlake, 1966). Furthermore, contrary to Gusfield's claims, America's alcohol prohibition illustrates that it is difficult to see a clear distinction between class conflict and status conflict, for both types of conflict involve the domination of the working class by higher social strata. In the United States class interests and conflict seem to infect even alcohol, opium, and marihuana prohibitions, situations in which one might imagine that class interests would be minimal, at least when compared with laws involving such issues as antitrust violations, legal control of factories, and other property rights.

Like Gusfield, Edelman (1964) found a symbolic role for law in American antitrust legislation. The mere passage of these laws in the late nineteenth century appeased Americans who were greatly concerned about the rapidly growing power and abuses of American corporations, even though these laws have in fact almost never been used to control business. Thus, Gusfield's (1967) distinction between instrumental and symbolic legislation seems inadequate to describe the legislative events that took place in antitrust legislation, since these unenforced, or symbolic, laws served the instrumental purpose of reassuring an angry public that past abuses of business leaders were no longer possible. Similarly, Carson's (1975) study of the origins of the United Kingdom's Factories Regulation Act of 1833 found both instrumental and symbolic origins for this legislation. Leading manufacturers had instrumental reasons for supporting this attempt to improve factory working conditions, including the possibility that these new requirements might force many smaller manufacturers out of business, thereby reducing competition. Yet initially these manufacturers were not enthusiastic about the legislation because of its symbolic significance, which appeared to condemn all manufacturers. Thus, Carson claims, "An exclusive empirical dichotomy between the two [instrumental and symbolic] is likely to be misleading . . . [since] most attempts to make law probably contain elements of both" (Carson, 1975: 136).

A parallel development was found in California's first opium law, passed in 1875, which used the symbol of moral inferiority as an instrument to divide the working class (Morgan, 1978). White workers were co-opted when the business community became convinced of their superiority to the Chinese. Once the labor market could no longer absorb both white and Chinese workers, the latter were accused of being immoral opium users who required stern criminal penalties to control their corrupt appetites. The 1875 law was aimed at removing the Chinese from the labor force and is associated historically with strict controls on Chinese immigration. Once the Chinese laborers were no longer needed, they lost the protection they had received earlier from members of the business community.

Other researchers have found that a symbolic role of law likewise applies to American marihuana prohibitions, which are routinely defended by legislators but, like alcohol prohibition laws before them, not usually enforced (Himmelstein, 1983). Still, Himmelstein observes, "Symbolic politics may also affirm domination of various kinds—economic, political, and ideological" (Himmelstein, 1983: 17). Galliher and Cross (1982, 1983) found, for example, that in the state of Nevada, where gambling and prostitution have been legal, the penalties for the possession of marihuana were the highest in the United States. While these high penalties were almost never enforced, local observers claimed the law was an effort of lawmakers to demonstrate, or symbolize, to others that, even with legal prostitution and gambling, Nevadans were not without some moral values. The state feared that federal interference could threaten the gambling industry, on which its economy has depended. Nevada's marihuana penalties, while seldom enforced, were thus seen as instrumental in protecting the state's reputation and hence its economy.

In sum, then, existing evidence of symbolic law is confounded by evidence of instrumentalism, perhaps because of the facts of social stratification in the societies thus far studied. If we are to locate an environment where purely symbolic legislation is enacted, it perhaps would have to be a society where social class is not so pervasively important as it is in the United States or the United Kingdom. In the Western world, it is difficult to locate a better candidate for this study than Iceland.

There is evidence that unenforced, symbolic legislation existed for over 70 years in Iceland in the form of beer prohibition, which was enacted in 1915. The prohibition of all other alcoholic drinks was soon abolished (wine in 1922 and other beverages in 1934). Moreover, "near beer" of 2.25 percent alcohol was legal, but on 10 occasions since 1932, proposals to increase the percentage to between 3.5 and 4.5 were defeated. The differences between the law and suggested alternatives were so modest that the continuing debate seems to reflect the operation of symbolic concerns rather than material interests.

Among the questions that can be raised about Iceland's beer prohibition are, What possible effect could such an isolated and minute prohibition have had on material well-being when all other alcoholic beverages were legally available for over 60 years? and What did this law indicate about Icelandic culture and social systems? More specifically, we will explore the question of whether this legislation represented purely symbolic politics, such as described by Gusfield, or whether it also contained instrumental qualities. In addition, we will examine how beer prohibition played a significant role in the unique Icelandic collective identity and boundary maintenance. Finally, we will demonstrate that the eventual repeal of beer prohibition was a consequence of Iceland's becoming increasingly opened up to the outside world.

The History of Prohibitionist Sentiment

On the basis of the results of a national referendum in 1908, the Parliament of Iceland voted in 1909 to cease the importation of all alcoholic beverages. At the time, this small nation had no domestic commercial brewing. Lawmakers believed that their actions made them the first nation in the Western world to pass such prohibition legislation. However, it was not until 1915 that a ban on sales went into effect, which provided a grace period between 1909 and 1915 designed to enable alcohol distributors to dispose of their remaining stocks. Complete prohibition remained in effect for only seven years, from 1915 until 1922. Even so, some discussion later arose in Parliament over the obvious consumption of alcohol during this period, which was presumed to involve illegal home-brewed beverages.

After the seven-year attempt at total prohibition, the law was modified as a result of economic pressures from the Spanish, who demanded that Iceland resume the importation of Spanish wine in return for the continued Spanish importation of Icelandic fish. Under such economic pressure, the Icelandic parliament agreed to except wine from its prohibition law.

Perhaps feeling uncomfortable with such a gerrymandered law, in 1928 Parliament decided that a national referendum should determine the future of prohibition, just as it had done in 1908. A referendum was finally conducted in 1933, and the majority of those who voted supported the repeal of prohibition. Given the exception already provided for Spanish wine, it seemed reasonable, at least to some members of Parliament, that other exceptions were plausible. In 1932 and 1933 two proposals were introduced in the lower house of Parliament to allow the brewing of beer with up to 4 percent alcohol. They were justified as attempts to abolish illegally brewed liquor, which was characterized as very harmful, especially when compared with beer, which was thought to be the least harmful of all alcoholic beverages. Local beer brewing, it was also argued, could prevent the loss of revenues through the importation of Spanish wine.

However, neither proposal succeeded because the opposition was formidable. For example, the chief physician of Iceland vigorously opposed the measures, arguing that beer would be especially harmful to the working class and the young, since "many workers and even children would tend to abuse beer because it's a relatively cheap substance" (Parliamentary Debates, 1932–1933: 1290). The prime minister also opposed this legislation, saying, "I totally disagree that consumption of beer is harmless; beer inevitably will evoke longing for alcohol, especially among youngsters, the working class, and students. It would be more useful even to allow importation of heavy liquor to Iceland than to allow brewing of beer" (Parliamentary Debates, 1932–1933: 1280–1281). Over the next 50 years these same arguments involving the defense of the young and workers would appear again and again.

The End of Prohibition and the Beginning of the Beer Battles

In 1934, legislation was introduced in Parliament to allow the importation of all alcoholic beverages. But the ban on local production of alcoholic beverages would remain in effect, with a separate provision, however, to allow the local brewing of beer if Parliament should approve it in a later separate vote. Proponents argued that beer brewing would both increase revenues to the state and create a successful profession for many Icelanders (*Morgunblaðið,* 1934). The opponents of the repeal of prohibition countered by saying that this argument revealed a serious inconsistency in the 1934 proposed bill, which in one place stated that the production of alcohol was prohibited but in another indicated the possibility of brewing beer. With the law's opponents capitalizing on this alleged inconsistency, the provision allowing for a later vote on beer brewing was expelled from the legislation.

Beer was thus singled out for special consideration almost by chance, first by pro-beer MPs and then by those opposed to alcohol, who seized on the alleged inconsistency to prevent a complete loss of prohibition. The final version of the bill, which was ultimately passed, allowed the importation of all alcoholic beverages except beer, which was still prohibited unless it contained less than 2.25 percent alcohol. One of the first, and certainly one of the most influential, to speak against ending the prohibition of beer was an MP who was both a farmer and a temperance leader. His argument that beer is an especially dangerous alcoholic beverage because it is used as a steppingstone to harder liquor would be used repeatedly over the next 50 years:

> The youth starts to drink beer and gets acquainted with the influence of alcohol. This develops step by step, the influence of beer becomes not enough, which leads to drinking strong liquor. But it is evident that beer evokes the longing for drinking alcohol. . . . Although we may allow the importation of strong liquor to Iceland, it is important to prohibit beer. . . . It's very important to prevent such a disaster, espe-

cially a disaster to the young people. (Parliamentary Debates, 1934–1935: 2110–2111)

A socialist member of Parliament also argued that working people in Iceland would be those most injured by beer and that they were especially vulnerable to its effects because of their Viking blood:

> Those with the lowest income, living under poor social conditions, have a great tendency to soothe their pain with alcohol drinking. . . . But why is alcohol legal? It is because alcohol production is a big profession, controlled by powerful capitalists and can't therefore be easily abolished. . . . The Parliament should be like a father to a child, knowing what is best for its welfare. . . . Poor people will start to drink beer, because it's the cheapest alcohol. But when beer has been consumed for a while, it leads to the consumption of hard liquor. (Parliamentary Debates, 1934–1935: 2157–2158, 2226)

A supporter of beer importation observed that it would be very strange to prohibit beer while allowing the importation of liquor, since beer is less harmful than other, stronger alcoholic beverages. This argument was used repeatedly by proponents of the end of beer prohibition for 50 years. In 1934 the new prime minister recalled that he had been the sheriff of Reykjavík, the capital of Iceland, when the importation of Spanish wine was resumed, and he had noticed no increase in the amount of drunkenness compared with the period before total prohibition, when all types of alcoholic beverages had been available. He added, "It's a strange regulation to prohibit brewing of beer, when importation of strong liquor has been allowed" (Parliamentary Debates, 1934–1935: 2093). However, during the debate the prime minister switched his position and soon spoke against legalizing beer (Parliamentary Debates, 1934–1935: 2237–2238). Paralleling his change of heart, the votes on the bill repealing prohibition in both houses were very lopsided, with the majority against the legalization of beer: 13 to 3 in the upper house and 24 to 8 in the lower house. It appears that the willingness of almost all in Parliament to exclude beer from the bill helped its passage, for this provision was used as a bargaining point between the opposing sides. The supporters of repeal apparently decided to compromise on the issue of beer to help ensure the passage of the rest of the bill.

The largest daily newspaper in Iceland, the *Morgunblaðið* in Reykjavík, strongly supported the repeal of prohibition, including the repeal of beer prohibition. There were 43 press reports on prohibition during the year prior to prohibition's partial repeal, many of which (37 percent) described home brewing and the accidents it caused. Some also described the total failure of prohibition in the United States. An article in the late fall of

1934 concluded that it made no sense to ban beer: "The ban of beer is ridiculous, everyone should understand that dangerousness of alcohol increases with alcohol content" (*Morgunblaðið*, 1934).

During the early phases of World War II the Icelandic parliament acted quickly and without debate, passing special legislation under an "emergency rule" (Parliamentary Debates, 1940–1941). This law allowed beer brewing for the British military forces, which had occupied Iceland just days before. Providing legal beer for foreigners was considered an emergency situation, although there was also clearly a profit motive.

In 1947 the beer issue surfaced again. A member of the lower house of Parliament introduced legislation to allow the local brewing of 4 percent beer as a means to decrease the consumption of hard liquor and to raise new tax revenues from domestic and export beer sales for building hospitals. The proposal was not taken seriously by most members of Parliament, and it did not come to a vote. Opponents capitalized on an apparent contradiction in the bill's objectives: to decrease alcohol consumption and at the same time to increase tax revenues from alcohol sales (Parliamentary Debates, 1946–1947: 196, 198).

Undaunted, in 1952 the proponents of beer were back again, in the upper house with a proposal for a national referendum on beer. However, this proposal was removed from suggested legislation by the minister of justice. It was at this time that opposition to a national referendum as a means of settling the beer issue first appeared. In 1953, as an indirect method of repealing the prohibition of beer, there was an effort in the upper house to limit the legal definition of alcohol to include only beverages with over 3.5 percent alcohol. There was considerable dispute as to how the bill, as worded, proposed to measure the percentage of alcohol in beer. Opponents claimed that the law proposed a new method of measuring alcohol content, whereas if the traditional method were used the actual alcohol level would be closer to 4.4 percent than to 3.5 percent. This alleged attempt at prohibition repeal was seen as a subterfuge and angered many MPs, especially in the lower house. It did not pass.

During the same session another bill was introduced in the lower house, this one to allow local brewing of 4.4 percent beer. The opponents of beer again capitalized on the apparent subterfuge in the earlier bill, and it was also defeated. Parliament did, however, pass legislation allowing alcohol to be brewed for export and for use on the NATO air force base in Keflavík, just as it had done for the British forces during World War II. It was argued that beer exports would help the economy, as had happened in Denmark and Holland, which were famous for their beers. There was apparently no moral concern about brewing beer for consumption by others, only concern about the effect on Icelanders. The newspaper published

32 articles on the beer issue in the year prior to the introduction of these two proposals and endorsed the suggestion of a national referendum (*Morgunblaðið*, 1953).

In 1954 a new government agency was created called the Council of the Government against Alcohol (CGAA). This agency is financed through taxes on alcohol sales, and its purpose is "to fight against abuse of alcohol and abolish the misfortune which follows abuse of alcohol" (alcohol law, no. 158, 1954, p. 169). In a 1984 interview with Helgi Gunnlaugsson, the manager of the CGAA explained the agency's opposition to the allowance of beer:

> There are several reasons why we oppose allowance of beer in Iceland. The most important one, however, is that experience in Iceland and other countries shows that any lenience in the alcohol law increases alcohol consumption in general. Thus, it is very likely that allowance of beer will not only be an addition to the present types of alcohol consumption in Iceland, but will also lead to an increased consumption on the whole. . . . We're no amateurs; we only provide scientific facts on the basis of reliable sources from different countries.

Over the years the CGAA has continued this line of reasoning, and its position has had a major impact on members of Parliament who frequently used this argument against the allowance of beer.

In 1960 another proposal for brewing beer with up to 3.5 percent alcohol content was introduced in the upper house with the rationale that the beer ban was "an insult to the Icelandic peoples' sense of liberty and civilization" (Parliamentary Debates, 1960–1961: 443). The bill's sponsor argued that brewing could help the economy through domestic beer sales and exportation, and also claimed that "people don't perceive they are violating the law [by making home-brewed beer] because prohibition of beer does not coincide with their sense of justice" (Parliamentary Debates, 1960–1961: 410). These arguments notwithstanding, the proposal was again defeated. The steppingstone argument surfaced again, as did the notion that beer is a special threat to workers. Another MP agreed, citing the horrible situation in the United Kingdom: "All factories and dock yards have to lock up their workers during working hours and especially take care to not let anyone out until the pubs are closed" (Parliamentary Debates, 1960–1961: 447). Yet another opponent told the following tale of woe: "A few days ago I witnessed a thirteen-year-old school boy saying that kids his age really needed beer to get up in the morning to go to school. This boy also believed it to be handy for the homes, because then they didn't have to bother about preparing coffee or tea, just grab the beer from the kitchen shelves" (Parliamentary Debates, 1960–1961: 438). Perhaps wearying of this issue to some extent, the *Morgunblaðið* devoted only 25 articles to the topic during the year prior to Parliament's deliberations. But the paper did editorialize, citing majority opinion and chemical reality: "It is a common fact that most people want to use alcohol, thus one immediately realizes how ridiculous it is to allow liquor but ban beer, which is healthier than liquor" (*Morgunblaðið*, 1960).

In 1965 a bill was introduced in the lower house to allow the brewing of 4.5 percent beer. The proposal was defeated, however, as was a proposal for a national referendum on beer. During the year prior, the *Morgunblaðið* had published 23 articles on beer, but seems to have given up on this issue and did not take an aggressive editorial position, as it had previously. Still, the paper did observe that "allowance of beer could become a major source of income for the state" (*Morgunblaðið*, 1965b). The paper also described a new brewery in northern Iceland with "perfect natural conditions for brewing beer" (*Morgunblaðið*, 1965a) and a Danish brewery that was very profitable and paid considerable taxes to the state (*Morgunblaðið*, 1966b). Three articles questioned a regulation, instituted by the minister of financial affairs in December 1965, that allowed ship and airplane crews to bring beer back to Iceland for their private use; it asked, "Why are seamen allowed to bring in beer, when it's not allowed here in Iceland?" (*Morgunblaðið*, 1966a). These crews could bring in up to 24 bottles of beer if they had been out of the country for less than 20 days, and 48 bottles if gone for over 20 days. Before the decision, this had been the informal practice for a number of years.

Three years later, in 1968, another national referendum was proposed, again in the lower house, but again defeated. In 1977 a national referendum was proposed in the lower house and then defeated once again. One MP later claimed that the beer issue was a "petty issue" and that it was therefore ridiculous to waste a national referendum on this proposition (Parliamentary Debates, 1983–1984c: 6387).

In parliamentary hearings during the late fall of 1983 a proposal for a national referendum on beer was introduced one more time, with the following preamble: "It sounds awfully strange to ban the sale of the weakest substance of all alcohol beverages, but allow sales of hard liquor. It sounds similar to a ban of aspirin, but allowance of morphine" (preamble to proposal no. 138, 1983–1984). This time the bill was introduced in both houses (Parliamentary Debates, 1983–1984a: 3335). In spite of these pleadings, the bill never came to a vote. Opponents argued that surveys were better measures of public opinion, and one said: "I doubt the usefulness of direct democracy like a national referendum, and I believe they don't have any future. In the Western world, a much better choice has appeared, attitude surveys, which are utilized to reveal the will of the people" (Parliamentary Debates, 1983–1984c: 3338). During these same hearings in the early spring of 1984, a proposal was introduced in the lower house to allow the local brewing and importation of beer, but the proposal was not discussed. Fifty-five articles on this issue had appeared in the *Morgunblaðið* during the prior year, with the newspaper supporting a national referendum. When it became apparent that the national referendum was to be defeated, a headline in the paper called it "Anti-Parliamentarian and Undemocratic Conduct" in Parliament (*Morgunblaðið*, 1984l).

Public Opinion and Party Politics

Nationwide surveys on the beer issue in Iceland indeed became increasingly common later in the twentieth century, and there was a steady increase in support for beer sales. In 1977, 57 percent opposed beer sales in Iceland (*DV*, 1977); in the summer of 1983, 53 percent wanted beer sales (Harðarson, 1983); and by the fall of 1983 the figure had risen to 63.5 percent (*Morgunblaðið*, 1983). Those most supportive of beer were the young and urban, with approximately 83 percent of those between the ages of 20 and 29 and 68 percent of those in the Reykjavík area supporting legal beer by 1983. In March 1984, 74 percent of all Icelanders surveyed supported the idea of a national referendum on the beer issue (*DV*, 1984).

Opponents of beer sales clearly distrusted direct democracy through referendums or even survey results. In our interviews in 1984, one member of Parliament complained about the press, perhaps thinking of Iceland's largest paper, which always supported the repeal of beer prohibition, for its distortion and manipulation of public opinion: "Nowadays, it is nothing but pure propaganda in newspapers that heavily influences people's minds. That's why so many support allowance of beer in these surveys, because papers carry so much propaganda for alcohol consumption. I believe, therefore, we should not take these surveys too seriously." Another added: "Propaganda of newspapers for increased consumption of alcohol has affected the public's mind. But I still believe that the majority of the public is against beer; surveys that indicate the opposite are most likely false." He said this even though he was the MP who had been quoted several months earlier during parliamentary debate as favoring surveys over a national referendum. One member of Parliament complained: "If a referendum is to be conducted, how should we protect the rights of the minority?"

An MP who was a supporter of a national referendum and legalized beer observed: "Opponents believe such direct democracy threatens their interests. There is also a strong distrust of voters, especially among MPs who come from rural areas." Proponents of legal beer cited the hypocrisy of allowing those who went abroad to bring in 12 half-liter cans of foreign beer or to purchase 24 bottles of Icelandic beer through the duty-free store upon reentering Iceland. The first privilege was allowed by the minister of financial affairs in 1979 and the second in 1984 after complaints were made about the unfair privileges of airplane and ship crews. Moreover, Iceland's bars sold a "beer" made by mixing the legal 2.25 percent "near beer" with liquor. During the early 1980s this practice was started in several Reykjavík bars, and the government prosecutor determined this to be legal, since both the 2.25 percent near beer and the whiskey were legal substances (*Morgunblaðið*, 1984k). The decision of the minister of financial affairs to allow travelers to bring in foreign beers or to purchase one case of Icelandic beer at the duty-free store for their personal use was nicely suited to permit the relatively affluent middle classes, who have the finances to travel abroad frequently, to have a steady supply of beer while denying it to the less affluent. This policy was consistent with the professed fear of the effect of beer upon workers. The deputy sheriff of Reykjavík discussed the impossibility of controlling beer consumption: "The police occasionally arrest people for brewing beer in their households. We find these people mostly through drunk drivers who maintain they've been drinking beer. But on the whole, we can do very little against this. Materials for brewing beer are sold everywhere legally" (August 1984 interview).

From the various parliamentary votes on the prohibition of beer over the years, it is clear that the Progressive Party, which has been predominantly rural, and the two socialist parties (Socialist Democratic Party and People's Alliance), which have traditionally represented workers, provided most of the opposition to beer proposals. Most of the support for beer came from the largest single political party, the Independence Party; with 38 percent to 42 percent of the vote, it has represented the urban middle class and has been endorsed by the *Morgunblaðið*. In the three actual votes on the issue of beer that took place, the Independence Party provided 73 percent of the support for beer proposals, and the socialists and the Progressives provided 80 percent of the opposition.

Economic and Demographic Foundations of Icelandic Law

The population of Iceland increased nearly threefold in the 60 years from 1910 to 1970, although farming and the rural areas of the country experienced rapidly declining numbers, with approximately half of the rural population lost in those years (see table 3.1). All these figures demonstrate that, although the urbanization process in Iceland began later than in the United States, it has been more rapid.

Table 3.1. Comparative demographic and economic characteristics of Iceland and the United States, 1910–1970

	1910	1930	1950	1970
	ICELAND			
Total population	85,183	108,861	143,973	204,578
Reykjavík area	17,595	37,188	70,648	119,822
Rural population	54,141	44,952	33,453	28,739
Work force				
Percent rural	63	42	23	14
Percent agricultural	48	35	24	12
Percent fishing	5	15	11	6
Percent industrial	12	20	32	37
	UNITED STATES			
Work force				
Percent rural	54	44	36	27
Percent agricultural	31	21	11	4
Percent industrial	28	24	29	27

Sources: Grímsson and Broddason, 1977: 153, 170; United States Department of Commerce, 1975: 11, 126–127, 137.

Table 3.1 also shows that in 1910 the area around the capital, Reykjavík, represented approximately only one-fifth of the nation's population, while in 1970 it represented over half of the total population. One reflection of how different the Reykjavík area is from the rest of the nation is that the next-largest city has less than a tenth of the country's population. This is an important distinction because, as we noted above, it was predominantly in the capital area that a majority desired to end beer prohibition.

The reapportionment of Parliament to reflect these remarkable population shifts was, however, slow in coming. In 1934 and again in 1959, Parliament reapportioned itself. But even so, the votes in rural Iceland clearly counted for more than those in urban areas. This is especially true in the capital even today, for while only 25 percent of Parliament is from the Reykjavík city proper, approximately 40 percent of the total population lives there. In 1908 and 1933 there were national referendums on alcohol, but not later. The unrepresentative nature of Parliament partly explains the growing reluctance of this body to rely on a direct referendum to settle the issue of beer or anything else. Thus even in such a small, ethnically, racially, and religiously homogeneous nation there has still been opposition to direct democracy.

Conclusions: Symbolic and Instrumental Law

It is curious that for all the appeal and apparent utility of the analysis of symbolic law, there have been only a few attempts to determine whether or how the idea of such law is applicable in other nations besides the United States (for example, see Carson, 1975). The implication of much of this research is that only Americans are so fundamentalist, puritanical, and shallow as to be pacified by such symbolic drug or alcohol legislation; certainly the generally more secular and sophisticated Europeans would not be so submissive. The goal of the present research has been to see if such an analysis could be useful in understanding legislative action in other than an American setting.

This case of beer prohibition in Iceland is especially interesting because elsewhere in the world beer has been less widely prohibited than hard liquor. This distinction is a result of the general recognition that beer is not as potent as other alcoholic beverages. However, some have claimed that beer is a steppingstone to hard liquor and therefore is especially dangerous to young people just beginning to drink, just as marihuana has often been alleged to be particularly dangerous as a steppingstone to the use of harder drugs among the young (Kaplan, 1970: 232; Himmelstein, 1983). The special irony is that in Iceland beer has been routinely associated with hard liquor, which has not been prohibited by law for over 60 years.

According to Gusfield's reasoning, it is very clear that the Icelandic beer law was an instance of symbolic legislation, because the difference in the alcohol content of legal near beer, compared with the proposed changes, ranged between only 1 percent and 2 percent. Moreover, beer was widely available in Iceland—ban or no ban. Those citizens who traveled abroad were allowed to bring in beer for their personal use; a "beer" composed of liquor and near beer was sold in some Reykjavík bars; and home-brewed beer has been widely made with no limitations on the percentage of alcohol, which is decided according to the preferences of the brewer. Beer prohibition was largely an unenforceable law, which Gusfield (1967) has claimed to be a sure indication of symbolic legislation, even though the proponents of the law argued that it served to control drinking behavior.

During the late nineteenth and early twentieth centuries, the United States was experiencing the rapid industrial expansion that would occur in Iceland approximately 50 years later. During this rapid American industrial development, national prohibition of alcohol was enacted, and juvenile codes and juvenile courts were created to deal with the problems of young people. These codes were a consequence of what has been called the child-saving movement (Platt, 1977). Although cloaked in the language of helping and protecting lower-class youth, such legislation was ideally suited to ensure that developing capitalism would in the future have the type of disciplined work force that it required. This same rationale was used in the United States for the defense of alcohol prohibition.

In the United States ethnic conflict has been related to class conflict, and both were associated with alcohol prohibition, which was opposed by labor unions. By comparison the temperance position of the socialist parties and the Icelandic labor unions, which represent workers in all industries, had their roots in the rapid industrialization of Iceland. Most Icelandic workers and union leaders have relatively recent rural origins and thus were opposed to alcohol. Moreover, some union leaders received their initial experience in political organizations through participation in the temperance movement (Einarsson, 1970: 32). In Iceland there are no minority ethnic groups, and there has been little economic stratification and class conflict. The country's labor unions originated in an attempt to imitate similar movements in western Europe and North America rather than because of local class conflict (Einarsson, 1970: 32; Kristjánsson, 1977). Since Iceland's labor unions were essentially borrowed from abroad rather than being created by local class conflict, these organizations came closer to representing status groups than class interests.

Like the "child savers" and prohibitionists in early twentieth-century America, the opponents of beer in Iceland continued to base their opposition to this substance for almost 70 years on its dreaded effects upon workers and young people, the workers of the future. Even though economic stratification and class conflict have not been pronounced in Iceland, one might get the opposite impression from the seemingly paternalistic references to the workers' special weaknesses and needs. Even the representatives of labor unions and the socialist parties repeatedly emphasized the weakness of the workers, the very people they represented, apparently because of Icelanders' "Viking blood." This gave an unexpected strength to the last vestiges of Icelandic prohibition. In contrast with the unions, the representatives of the urban middle class have always seen beer and other alcohol simply as commodities to be exploited for the income they can generate for industry, employment, and tax revenues for the state.

Rural Icelanders began losing their numerical strength in the middle of the century, just as rural American Protestants did earlier. Yet rural Icelanders maintained some sense of power through the law in an unrepresentative parliament, and, in the instance of beer prohibition, they had the support of the political parties of the workers and unions. Beer prohibition was thus a means of demonstrating rural domination in the face of population odds attendant to the rapid changes that have occurred in Iceland's economic and social system. Such a protracted conflict in Icelandic politics has obscured class, or material, interests because during most of this century there has been only the most rudimentary class system in the country (Tomasson, 1980: 195). Since economic stratification developed much later in Iceland compared with other Western democracies, in the past its parliament was easily deflected from material issues to status conflicts. Industrialization likewise came later than in other Western countries and developed much more rapidly because of the influence of these other nations. The rural domination of Parliament, its beer prohibition, and the prohibitionist sentiment of labor unions were dramatic reflections of the resulting cultural lag.

The ambiguous mixture of class and status conflict that existed in the American prohibition movement, in which the alcohol-status conflict seemed closely aligned with the class conflict between capitalists and workers, was absent from beer prohibition in Iceland. Unlike the case of American prohibition, in Iceland the middle class clearly wanted no prohibition laws forced upon workers and did not accept the logic of workers' special vulnerability to alcohol. Thus Iceland's beer prohibition had its foundations in the local social structure that created the conditions for social conflict between rural citizens and workers on the one hand and the urban middle class on the other. This particular conflict differed from conventional class conflict because in Iceland a rural working-class coalition controlled the urban middle class. This suggests an urban-rural status conflict unlikely to be found in most other Western nations.

Most of the studies of symbolic law reviewed above recognized the importance of the perception of actors involved in these legislative events. There were discussions of the perceptions of Nevada lawmakers (Galliher and Cross, 1982, 1983), English manufacturers (Carson, 1975), American corporate leaders (Edelman, 1964), and white workers and business leaders in California during the late nineteenth century (Morgan, 1978). All these studies, to some degree, show a business group operating according to class interests. While Timberlake (1966) found influential business interests in the case of American prohibition, Gusfield (1955, 1963, 1967) missed any instrumental qualities in the perceptions of the WCTU members he interviewed. But just as surely as American prohibitionists believed in the positive effects of the law they advocated, proponents of beer prohibition in Iceland remained firmly convinced of its instrumental qualities in controlling drinking behavior and thus struggled unceasingly on its behalf. Surely social scientists can all agree with the time-honored dictum that if people believe a thing to be true, it is real in its consequences. And so it was with alcohol prohibition in both the United States and Iceland.

Moreover, Icelandic beer prohibition probably did make the substance more difficult to secure, for beer was either home-brewed or imported in small amounts. Prohibition supporters understandably believed that Icelanders drank less because of beer prohibition. Therefore, even the extreme case of beer prohibition in Iceland, while it was clearly not the result of class conflict, was still something other than a totally symbolic law. Making the distinction between the instrumental and symbolic origins of law, as Gusfield (1955, 1963, 1967) has done, seems inadequate because no laws appear to have totally symbolic origins, even in Iceland, where status conflict rather than class conflict has been the norm. As late as 1985, beer prohibition in Iceland showed no sign of ending. During the summer of 1985 a bill to allow the importation and brewing of beer and one to authorize a national referendum on the prohibition were introduced. As with all earlier bills of these types, both were defeated.

Postscript: Eventual Legalization

Beer prohibition was finally abolished by Parliament in May of 1988 and the new law allowing beer sales took effect in March 1989. Prior to the passage of the new law, proposals to allow beer brewing and sales or to let a public referendum settle the issue had been introduced in Parliament each year since the parliamentary session of 1983–1984. The proposals were always hotly debated but were postponed, ending in committee or defeated in a vote in Parliament, before finally being passed in 1988.

In 1985 the lower house passed a proposal allowing beer sales, but the upper house passed an amendment that a referendum should first settle the issue before Parliament finally decided on it. The lower house had, however, earlier defeated such a proposal; those who supported beer sales argued that beer opponents in the upper house were now supporting a referendum as a delaying tactic. The issue of a referendum was then defeated again in the lower house (Parliamentary Debates, 1984–1985).

Another proposal was introduced in 1986, now with beer proponents adding a referendum. The sponsors admitted that they were not in favor of a referendum, since they believed that Parliament should settle the issue and that the majority of MPs were actually in favor of a repeal of the beer ban. Yet keeping in mind the fate of the issue the year before, they argued that this time they were adding the referendum to the proposal to ensure its passage. The upper house, however, defeated the proposal, which supported the allegation, made by those who favored beer sales, that beer opponents were able to block its passage in Parliament by supporting a referendum on the issue when a passage of beer sales seemed imminent and then defeating the idea when such a solution was introduced by beer proponents. It appeared that those MPs who favored beer sales were divided on the idea of a referendum. Some wanted Parliament to settle the issue, whereas others believed it also to be appropriate to let the electorate decide the issue. Beer opponents apparently took advantage of this split among those who favored beer sales and were therefore able to stop its passage (Parliamentary Debates, 1985–1986).

In 1987 another proposal was introduced and debated, with one MP who supported beer sales arguing that no other issue had been as hotly debated in Parliament (Parliamentary Debates, 1987–1988a; *Morgunblaðið*, 1987). Then the proposal was forwarded to committee for comments, but in February 1988 yet another proposal was introduced that the majority of the committee believed to be easier to pass. This case was, as always before, a hot issue in society, and many groups outside Parliament were asked to submit commentary on the beer proposal. Most notable was a group of professors of medicine at the University of Iceland and detox physicians, who requested that Parliament defeat this proposal, implicitly arguing that the science of medicine was against beer. In turn, a total of 133 specialized medical doctors submitted another statement: "It is likely that consumption of alcoholic beverages (with allowance of beer) would be geared more towards weaker alcoholic beverages instead of stronger ones" and that there was no causal relationship between total consumption of alcohol in society and the number of alcoholics (Parliamentary Debates, 1987–1988b).

When the passage of this proposal seemed imminent, beer opponents once again came up with an amendment involving a referendum, which was, however, defeated in a close vote in the lower house. Then the lower house passed a bill allowing beer brewing and sales, 23 to 17. The upper house also passed the proposal, 13 to 8 (*Morgunblaðið*, 1988). Finally, the beer battle came to an end after the brew had been banned since 1915. The arguments either for or against beer sales did not change much from previous debates. Opponents still argued that alcohol consumption would increase with its dreaded effects on users, and those who favored beer sales pointed to the oddity of the law allowing liquor but banning beer and noted that drinking habits might be actually improved with allowance of beer.

Why did the beer ban end in 1988, not sooner or later? Both internal and external factors contributed to this timing. First, support for beer sales among the general population had become more apparent in the 1980s, both in the capital and in other areas, and this exerted considerable pressure on Parliament to lift the ban. Moreover, allowing only those who traveled abroad the privilege of purchasing beer while denying it to others was increasingly felt to be discriminatory and unjust. Selling beer to customers of bars by mixing liquor with near beer also seemed to highlight the oddity of the law.

Opposition to beer had traditionally been found among MPs from rural areas and the socialist parties, but with an increase in both support for beer sales and urbanization, this division gradually diminished. Icelandic society had been radically transformed from earlier in the century (Gunnlaugsson and Bjarnason, 1994). By 1990, about 90 percent of the population lived in urban areas, with an occupational structure similar to that found in other Western nations. Reinforced by local and worldwide events, the nation had been transformed in only a matter of decades from a country relying on subsistence farming into a Scandinavian-style welfare state with an industrial economic base. Parliament was slow in reapportioning itself to reflect these remarkable population shifts. When the beer bill was passed in 1988 approximately 38 percent of the population lived in Reykjavík, while only about 29 percent of MPs represented the capital. Still, this was a closer representation of actual population shifts than had been true earlier. As before, most of the support for beer sales in the final vote came from the Independence Party, but now the majority of the rural Progressive Party, in stark contrast with earlier beer votes, also supported beer sales. A small majority of the two socialist parties still opposed beer sales. Rural and urban MPs did not differ significantly (see Steinsson, 1996).

As for the idea of a national referendum, it is a very rare phenomenon in Icelandic politics and did not have much support among those who favored beer sales and probably not even among those who opposed beer sales. For opponents of beer sales, the idea of a referendum was probably more an instrument to block the passage of a beer proposal than a genuine proposal. But in 1965 and 1968 those who favored beer sales were more willing to let a referendum settle the issue because it was probably evident to them that a repeal of the ban did not have a majority in Parliament, since Parliament had not yet been adequately reapportioned to reflect the population shifts. It is likely that the idea of a referendum threatens mostly those who represent smaller constituencies, and given the overrepresentation of rural areas in Parliament, the idea of a referendum must have been less tempting to them. Yet, this difference could not be detected in the final votes on beer in 1988. Both sides seemed equally opposed to the idea of a referendum.

Moreover, external factors also help explain the repeal of the beer ban. The worldwide internationalization has only gradually and recently broken the isolation of Iceland. In 1950 when the Icelandic population was about 150,000, only about 4,300 Icelanders traveled abroad and about 4,400 foreigners visited Iceland. In 1970, the numbers had increased to about 27,000 Icelanders traveling abroad and 53,000 foreigners visiting Iceland. In 1988, when beer was finally allowed, about 150,000 Icelanders traveled abroad, or more than two-thirds of the whole population. As for foreigners visiting Iceland in 1988, the number had risen to approximately 130,000. These numbers have continued to increase in recent years, and in 1995 about 166,000 Icelanders traveled abroad and more than 200,000 foreigners visited Iceland in 1996 (Icelandic Tourist Board, 1996). This clearly suggests that the geographical isolation of Iceland has been broken, and a substantial part of the Icelandic population has traveled abroad and become acquainted with other drinking customs taken for granted in most of the Western world. Thus by the 1980s most Icelanders had first-hand experience with legal beer in most other countries. They knew that legal beer did not necessarily have dreaded effects and that Iceland's prohibition was both an oddity and based on questionable assumptions.

Other changes that point to modernization and more liberalized alcohol policies have taken place as well. In 1954, only one restaurant in Iceland had a license to serve alcohol. In 1980, the number had increased to 37 restaurants, and in 1988 when the ban on beer was finally lifted the number had increased to 148. In 1994 the number stood at 322 restaurants with a license to serve alcoholic beverages (Steinsson, 1996: 138). The same development can also be detected in the number of state monopoly liquor stores. In 1962, only 7 liquor stores could be found in the entire nation, but in 1994 the number had risen to 24 (State Alcohol and Tobacco Monopoly, annual reports, 1962, 1994).

What impact have liberalized alcohol policies had on the total consumption of alcoholic beverages in Iceland? If we look at statistics from the Icelandic State Alcohol and Tobacco Monopoly, consumption of alcohol has indeed increased in recent decades. In 1966, the total consumption of alcohol was 2.33 liters per capita; in 1976 the consumption was 2.88 per capita; and in 1988, the year before the repeal of the beer ban went into effect, the consumption had increased to 3.35 liters. In 1990, the consumption had increased to 3.93 liters, about a 15 percent increase over the consumption in 1988. But beer consumption has been increasing while consumption of stronger alcoholic beverages has decreased. According to these statistics, Icelanders still consume less alcohol than most Western nations (World Drink Trends, 1996; State Alcohol and Tobacco Monopoly, annual report, 1993). Abolition of beer seems, therefore, not to have had a great impact on the amount of alcohol consumed in Iceland and clearly suggests the symbolic nature of the ban. Even so, the loss of beer prohibition required the development of new vehicles for boundary maintenance, nicely filled, we will later see, by a war on drugs.

4

Crime Stories in the Icelandic Press

There are at least two views of the relationship between crime and the mass media. One is that the media merely reflect the level of crime and the fear of it in the community. The other view is that the public's fear of crime is a result of manipulation by journalists and government officials. For example, Fishman (1978) has demonstrated that media "crime waves" are artificial creations of law enforcement, the press, and politicians. Law enforcement officials typically know when the media want particular types of stories and supply them whenever possible. On the other hand, political officials often have the power to stop the press from pursuing certain types of crime reporting. Thus a symbiotic relationship develops among the press, politicians, and law enforcement officials which can distort the image of crime presented to the community. Indeed, in a pioneering study of crime reporting, Davis (1952) found an inverse relationship between crime rates and the amount of crime reporting. We will show that in Iceland, press reporting in general has accurately reflected the amount of crime in the community, except for drugs and violence. Media reporting of crime in this small homogeneous nation generally represents the common perception of the media, the government, and citizens as a whole. Yet just as in other nations, in Iceland sensational reporting and dramatic stories on drugs and violence are appealing to the press in its efforts to sell its papers and attract readers. Newspapers can be expected to be especially influential in a nation such as Iceland, with its high levels of literacy and commitment to reading. We will see how increasing alarm is spread throughout the land by press reports about the threat of crime, violence, and drug abuse.

News Reports of Crime

In order to gain some insight into the public perceptions of crime in Iceland, we reviewed crime-related articles in the *Morgunblaðið* (all the

48

source citations in this chapter pertain to this publication unless otherwise noted), the most widely read daily newspaper in the nation, with a circulation of over 50,000 among approximately 272,000 citizens. Approximately 60 percent of the population read the paper daily. This newspaper is read in virtually every part of the country and takes pride in being the nation's paper with an objective approach to newsworthy events. To supplement the rather sketchy government crime reports, we will use information on the frequency and prominence of crime reporting.

The review includes all newspapers from 1969, 1974, 1979, 1984, 1989, and 1993. The reason for selecting 1969 as the starting point is that this was the year when the first drug seizure occurred in Iceland. After starting with this year, we proceeded in mostly five-year intervals. In 1973 a separate drug court was established, and our review of the 1974 newspapers should shed some light on this court's early operations. Also, in 1984 there was a highly unusual parliamentary investigation into the methods of the nation's legal processing of sex offenses, and in 1989 there was a spate of violent crime in the nation's capital. Presumably, our newspaper review should help us understand these events.

Crime Reports in 1969

As table 4.1 indicates, there were 239 crime-related news reports in the *Morgunblaðið* in 1969. Most of these reports were minor, neither lengthy nor prominently placed. Still, crime reports were frequent, appearing in almost every issue of the paper, primarily on the second page, which is devoted to domestic affairs, or on the back page.

Property crimes for this year involved a number of kinds of offenses, including burglaries and fraud. Stories of this type were by far the most common, constituting nearly two-thirds of the total. The bulk of these cases involved adolescents engaged in burglaries of stores and homes. The headlines are suggestive: "Musical Instruments Stolen" (1969b), "12-Year-Old Burglars" (1969h), and "Stole His Grandmother's Freezer" (1969c). A notable exception to these relatively minor property crimes were four news reports on white-collar offenses. A candy manufacturer was ordered by the Supreme Court to pay a large fine for failure to pay taxes and customs expenses (1969a), a person was charged with forgery (1969d), and an accountant was sentenced to a year in prison for embezzlement, fraud, and illegal bookkeeping practices (1969e).

The sex crimes in 1969 involved rape and child molesting. The homicide category primarily involved reporting on one murder (seven out of nine stories) from the year before, when a taxi driver was shot to death in his cab. The killer was never apprehended, although reports discussed the

Table 4.1. Numerical and percentage distributions of newspaper crime reports, by type of offense, for various years from 1969 to 1993

	1969		1974		1979		1984		1989		1993		Total	
	n	%	n	%	n	%	n	%	n	%	n	%	N	%
Property crimes	157	65	130	47	99	36	119	52	100	38	158	39	763	45
Homicide	9	4	36	14	34	12	9	4	6	2	7	2	101	6
Sex crimes	9	4	13	5	19	7	14	6	26	10	38	9	119	7
Other violence	12	5	28	10	8	3	26	11	39	15	58	14	171	10
Drugs	16	7	17	6	68	24	40	18	52	20	50	12	243	14
Arson	2	1	7	3	8	3	3	1	6	1	11	3	37	2
Other crimes	34	14	45	16	41	15	18	8	37	14	87	21	262	16
Totals	239	100	276	100	277	100	229	100	266	100	409	100	1,696	100

Source: All issues of the Morgunblaðið for the years shown.

murder weapon, which had been located, and indicated that one suspect was held in custody for a time.

Drug-related reports involved 7 percent of the total. Although not frequent in number, these stories were prominently reported and given more space than other crime news. Two stories involved drugs being found in Iceland's largest prison. There were also reports of drugs being seized in Denmark and West Germany, several reports involving the United States, and others involving an American soldier suspected of distributing drugs to an Icelander. One story focused on new equipment used by Icelandic customs authorities to locate drugs carried by air passengers (1969f). Reports on drug use among Icelanders began to heat up in the fall: "Suspicion that adolescents use hashish" (1969g), "though such substances have never been found among passengers to Iceland. . . . Customs officials increase their control to suspend all doubts." Soon the suspicion of drug use among adolescents was confirmed by a headline (1969i): "Adolescents Found Using Drugs." This incident involved three youths, two 14-year-old girls and a 15-year-old boy, who confessed to having used LSD, marihuana, and hashish. They were subjected to intense questioning by the police, and the boy admitted to having purchased the drugs in a movie theater but could tell the police nothing more about the drugs' origins.

On 18 November two drug-related stories appeared: one reprinted from an American story about children and drugs, and another with the headline "Arrested with Hard Drugs" (1969j), involving five Icelanders (18 to 20 years old) apprehended at a Reykjavík party. One of those arrested had been arrested earlier in Copenhagen and expelled from Denmark, apparently smuggling a "white substance" with her when she returned to Iceland. The police believed "there are more such cases going on among us and these matters are taking a dangerous turn." Two days later a follow-up report on this incident indicated that the seized substance had been sent abroad for further analysis to determine its exact nature (1969k). To emphasize how serious these events were perceived to be, an editorial appeared on 16 December observing: "This has not been a problem here in Iceland, which is why there is no legislation concerning drugs. The Parliament needs to pass a law where stiff penalties are adopted" (1969l). And finally on 19 December, a conference to be sponsored by the Youth Council of Iceland was announced for early 1970 to deal with "drug use among youth" (1969m).

The "other crimes" category included reports of traffic-related violations (such as DWIs), illegal alcohol brewing, a planned new prison, escapes from prison, vandalism, and the smuggling of various goods into Iceland. In general, although news reports of crime were frequent, they were usually very short stories and were not given prominent coverage by the press. There were, however, four editorials on crime: one dealing with the danger of drugs, one on youth vandalism, and two on the need for prison reform. While drug-related stories were not frequent, this new problem was viewed with great alarm by the press, which was reflected in the space and prominence given to such reports.

Crime Reports in 1974

The total number of crime-related stories in 1974 increased to 276, slightly more than the 1969 total (see table 4.1). However, it must be noted that there was a one-and-a-half-month newspaper strike between 25 March and 10 May, when no newspapers were published. Compared with 1969, the number and proportion of property crime articles had now decreased, whereas the number and proportion of reports of violence had increased. Now, more than in 1969, the paper collapsed several minor property offenses into one news report instead of reporting them separately.

This growing concern with violence could have been expected, since we saw in chapter 2 that official reports showed parallel increases in homicides at this time. Even so, the number of reports involving homicide is surprisingly high, with 36 such news articles. These stories involve eight cases of homicide, with 20 articles devoted to one case. Reporting on this case began late in the year (1974c) and was frequently in the news until year's end. The case involved a missing person from Keflavík who suddenly disappeared without a trace, after which rumors spread that the person had been killed. This later became known as the case of Geirfinnur and became very controversial and gained high media attention. The case was not concluded until 1980, when the Supreme Court sentenced three persons to 8-, 16-, and 17-year prison sentences for the murder of Geirfinnur and another victim linked to the case. Neither of the bodies was ever found. Most of the stories surrounding this case were relatively lengthy. Additional stories on violence were primarily those involving assaults (n = 28). One article observed that there was a wave of violence taking place in Iceland (1974d), reflected in six homicide cases during the previous few months. This number is surprisingly high compared with the average of just over three homicides per year between 1972 and 1974.

Even with the collapsing of reports of numerous property crimes into one article, these are by far the most common crime news stories, with approximately one such report for every two issues of the paper. These cases typically involved minor burglaries and other thefts, including 11 articles on auto theft. The 13 sex-crime stories included 8 stories of rape or attempted rape. One story reflected the stereotype of the violent stranger-rapist. Here the offenders forced entry into a private home, knocked down the husband, and raped the wife (1974b). The low number of sex-crime reports corresponds well with the low number found in court statistics, which represented approximately 2 percent of the total convictions. Although few in number, these sex-crime reports were given prominent coverage in the paper and discussed in relatively lengthy stories.

There were 17 drug-related crime news stories, and most of these involved cannabis. Only one story involved LSD. We will see later that this corresponds closely with the types of cases handled by the narcotics police. A few reports involved foreigners, mostly soldiers from the NATO base at Keflavík. The seven drug-related reports involving Icelanders typically were on the back page of the paper and always involved more than one person. In one of these cases the quantity of drugs seized was substantial, totaling several kilos of cannabis (1974a). In 1974 during the first full year of operation of a special drug court, the number of cases processed totaled 171 and represented a sharp increase from the previous year. The category of "other crimes" includes vandalism (n = 16), violations of territorial waters (n = 11), and smuggling and illegal brewing (n = 10), as well as several other articles. In 1974 the most frequent crime news stories continued to be property offenses, which were not emphasized in the press by length or prominent placement.

Crime Reports in 1979

The total number of crime-related stories was virtually the same in 1979 as it was in 1974. There was a decrease in the number of stories dealing with property crimes. In 1979 there was less emphasis in the press on relatively minor crime and greater concentration on other offenses, including business-related crimes and drug offenses. Reports on drug offenses jumped from 16 in 1969, and 17 in 1974, to 68 in 1979. Reports on drug-related crimes were usually prominently displayed on the second page or on the back page of the newspaper.

Almost a third of the property-crime reporting was business related (n = 28). The most noteworthy case involved four articles concerning a bank department head who was found to have systematically embezzled large sums from the largest bank in Iceland over a seven-year period (1979b). Other news involved fraud by auto dealers and by the owners of a cargo shipping line. Another noteworthy case was an alleged armed robbery at a post office in a small village, where the offender wore a mask and threatened the clerk with what was eventually reported to have been a toy gun (1979e). Four stories appeared about this case. Although the offender was never found, there were some humorous but promising leads. The clerk recalled that the robber had used Old Spice shaving lotion, and the director of the post office had dreams about the robbery prior to its occurrence. There were eight stories on auto theft.

Sex-crime reporting increased in frequency from previous years, with 12 rape cases discussed in a total of 19 reports. One defendant was sentenced to a year in prison for rape and another received a two-year sentence (1979h). There were infrequent reports of arrests for incest, child molesting, and possession of pornographic materials. Even though sex crimes were not frequently reported, those that were reported were usually prominently printed with large headlines reflecting their perceived significance. This same year there were 21 reports of rape to the State Criminal Investigative Police (Rape Report, 1989: 137), or nearly twice the number reported in the press.

There were 34 articles on homicide reported in the press, involving four separate cases. Possibly the most notorious of these was a case where one member of a rock band killed another band member (1979k). The prison sentences for these four homicide convictions were: 16 years, 14 years, 7 years, and 9 months. On 18 January (1979d) it was reported that there had been 14 cases of homicide in the past seven years and 38 since the beginning of the century. Reporting on other nonlethal violence decreased in frequency and generally involved stabbings. Illustrative cases included a landlord who wounded his tenant and an assault by a husband on his wife.

Approximately a fourth of all reports involved drug offenses, with two especially sensational cases covered by 38 articles. In Copenhagen in early spring (1979f), several Icelanders were arrested and stood accused of trafficking in cocaine worth up to $1 million. The *Morgunblaðið* sent a reporter to Denmark to cover the story, and two full pages were devoted to this case (1979g). The paper followed the case for the next two months until prison sentences were meted out to the three principal offenders— three months, six months, and three years. The other case began in Gothenburg, Sweden (1979j), and involved eight Icelanders arrested for selling hashish. Twelve stories appeared on this case. Two stories concerned a pair of Icelanders who were imprisoned because of smuggling hashish into West Germany (1979a, c).

It might come as a surprise that the paper devoted so much attention to drug cases abroad. It must be kept in mind that these cases involved Icelanders, and they could one day return to Iceland to continue their alleged drug trafficking. Whatever Icelanders do abroad is always of local interest. A noteworthy news story on the drug situation in Iceland appeared late in the year (1979l). A full page was devoted to a lengthy interview with the deputy director of the drug police, in which he stated that the drug problem in Iceland "has escalated in recent years and more police manpower and education about drugs are needed to combat this problem," especially in view of the growth of heroin trafficking and indoor growing of marihuana. He stated in the interview that, since the creation of the drug police, a total of 4,000 young people had been implicated in their drug investigations, that young people had died because of drug use, and that heroin had made its entry into Iceland. "Other crime" stories included smuggling, traffic violations including DWIs, and illegal brewing.

Crime Reports in 1984

Although the 229 crime-related articles published in the paper represented a decline from previous years, crime reporting still generally occurred on a daily basis, the distortion in the relative numbers being attributable to another strike from 10 September to 20 October, when the paper was not published. And property-crime reporting still led all other types of stories, with drug-related articles in second place. Three cases were responsible for 42 of the property-crime stories. The case drawing the greatest attention (20 articles) involved a West German couple who were caught in Iceland with eight stolen falcon eggs intended for resale in West Germany (1984i). The husband was given a steep fine and a few months in prison, but he disappeared and was believed to have fled back to West Germany and thus never served his sentence. Thirteen news stories covered three men suspected of robbing banks in Reykjavík. They had threatened a cashier, who then gave them a considerable sum of money. They were soon caught and given 5 years, 18 months, and 6 months in prison (1984o). The third case also involved an armed robbery and was the subject of nine stories. Two men with a stolen shotgun robbed a liquor store in Reykjavík, firing at a vehicle as they drove away (1984e). Less than a week later they were apprehended.

While rape stories this year continued to be low in frequency, one incident in Reykjavík (1984m) caused Parliament to pass a resolution to form a committee to investigate possible reforms in the manner in which sex crimes were handled by the legal system. This initiative by Parliament was pressed by the Women's Alliance Party, and in 1989 the committee issued its findings, referred to as *Skýrsla nauðgunarmálanefndar* (the Rape Report). The incident in question involved a 36-year-old male, with no prior criminal record, who attacked two women. After he had been held in custody for less than 24 hours and police had finished their preliminary investigation, the offender was released by the Reykjavík Criminal Court. This decision was, however, criticized by both the police and the public prosecutor. Ultimately the defendant was sentenced to a four-year prison term (1984r), one of the stiffest rape sentences ever handed down. Nine out of 14 sex-crime news reports this year were devoted to this case.

As for homicide articles, the paper reported on one case (1984c) and had follow-up stories on the sentencing for four murders occurring prior to 1984. One of the cases originally occurring prior to 1984 was the "case of

Geirfinnur." As already noted, the alleged killing occurred in 1974 and the paper now noted, "Those who were convicted have all been released on parole after having served half of their prison sentences" (1984s). The crime reporting in the category of "other violence" increased this year, with approximately 11 percent of all articles dealing with such cases. And over half of these involved one of the following three cases: a crazed gunman who was arrested for shooting wildly in Reykjavík (1984j), a brawl between two neighbors (1984q), and a follow-up on a story of alleged brutality against a disco patron by the disco bouncer and the police (1984d). The paper on 15 March concluded in an editorial: "There is no doubt that increasing use of cannabis and other drugs is a major contributing factor to increased violence in Iceland. Stiffer penalties are required, as is more education in the schools about the effects of drugs" (1984h).

Indeed, drug reports were a frequent source of news with 40 articles on the topic this year. Seven of these articles reported on conferences for the public on the dreaded effects of drugs, one of which was organized by a political party. Wiretapping was used in drug cases, for "by law a judge can permit wiretapping when the security of the state requires it or when there are major criminal cases" (1984b). The paper agreed that these drug offenses were major criminal cases, strongly stating its position in one of two anti-drug editorials that year: "Penalties should be stiffened, as this is so serious and condemnable behavior that it is not possible to justify a soft approach. . . . [And] four tons of hashish are believed to be used in Iceland per year" (1984a). A member of Parliament was so outraged that he proclaimed: "We need more than anything else to exterminate this disgrace, find those bastards who are behind the smuggling of drugs for monetary reasons, changing children into wretches in a relatively short period of time" (1984f). Two drug cases received particular attention. The first involved a drug seizure by the police on an Icelandic ship. Four people were arrested and accused of attempting to smuggle 700 grams of amphetamines and 400 grams of hashish oil (1984n). The other case involved the smuggling of 226 doses of LSD and 100 grams of amphetamines and cocaine, "The Largest Case Involving LSD Ever" (1984u). A total of six news reports were devoted to these two cases, most very prominently placed in the paper and given considerably more space than other crime reports.

The last category of crime reporting, "other crimes," consisted of traffic violations, with five articles devoted to drunk driving and three stories each devoted to arson, smuggling, and prison escapes. In this category is another noteworthy report describing the findings of a Gallup opinion survey that had just been completed in Iceland (1984t). One finding was that the public had more confidence in the police than in any other public institution and that, as a nation of peaceful people, the vast majority (90 percent) would never use violence as a means of achieving their political objectives.

Crime Reports in 1989

As table 4.1 indicates, there were 264 crime-related news reports in 1989, which was very close to the number in 1974 and in 1979. Notable changes from earlier years included continuing decreases in property-crime reporting. Homicide reports were relatively rare, with only six such articles. There was a corresponding increase in articles about drug crimes, sex crimes, and other violence. Sex-related crime stories represented 10 percent of the total. These stories involved a total of eight rapes and the sentencing of a man to six months for pandering (1989f). Reporting on violent crimes, other than cases involving sex offenses or homicide, was more frequent than in previous years. A total of 21 of these articles appeared in the last four months of the year, when a violent crime wave was alleged to have hit downtown Reykjavík (1989g), with 11 articles in December alone. This alleged crime wave prompted the chief of police to comment, "We need more police officers to ease the burden" (1989g). In response to this turn of events the city government passed a resolution providing for increased policing in the downtown area (1989i). Actually, most of these cases involved scuffles between young people gathering in the downtown area at night, including "nine reports of woundings over the weekend with two being seriously injured" (1989h). Later, it was suggested that cameras be installed in the area and that police officers patrol with dogs (1989k). These ideas, however, were not implemented at the time. By the late 1990s, cameras were installed. The "other crimes" category covers topics ranging from smuggling to drunk driving, bootlegging, and prison escapes.

Drug reporting was frequent with a total of 52 such news stories. Two cases received the most attention, both of which involved cocaine. One involved five articles that covered the case of two persons who were arrested in downtown Reykjavík for importation and intention to sell 56 grams of the drug (1989b). The other case was mentioned in 14 news articles and involved two people who were arrested for attempting to smuggle one kilo of cocaine from the United States. This was referred to as the biggest drug case in Iceland's history (1989d). The principal offender was held in custody for seven months, during the initial investigation (1989j). By Icelandic standards this seven months represented an unusually long period of confinement and was a consequence of the alleged offender's total denial of any responsibility for the crime, despite testimony to the contrary from several other sources that he was the principal offender.

Other noteworthy drug-crime articles included a report of the confiscation of 700 doses of LSD from a Reykjavík home (1989c) and the seizure of 4 to 5 kilos of hashish at the Keflavík airport (1989e). An investigator assigned to the drug police was interviewed by the press (1989a) about the drug situation in Iceland. He claimed that his agency had information indicating that the methods of smuggling drugs into Iceland were becoming much more sophisticated and that the use of hard drugs was becoming much more widespread, but he admitted that the exact dimensions of these problems "had not been mapped out."

Crime Reports in 1993

As table 4.1 shows, there was a dramatic increase in the number of crime articles in 1993 compared with previous years. The total of 409 crime articles that year represents an increase of about a third from 1989. The number of "other crimes" increased, and they included DWIs, illegal brewing, and public drunkenness. Property crimes consisted primarily of burglaries, and an editorial on the subject titled "Crime Epidemic" (1993e) expressed concern and urged action against burglaries, claiming that the situation in Reykjavík was becoming like any other major city in the world. On the heels of the editorial was a news report revealing that insurance companies had to pay a total of $1.5 million in compensation because of burglaries in 1992 (1993f).

As for homicide, one report noted that a male had been given a five-year prison sentence for attempted manslaughter (1993d). The most infamous sex crime involved a male who received a 10-year prison sentence and a $40,000 fine for victim compensation for two rapes, an assault, and a robbery (1993i). A DNA test was used to prove his guilt. As for other violence, a news report noted that wounds inflicted by violence had increased about 20 percent since 1980, according to the city of Reykjavík's hospital records (1993l). Another report involved a man who had received an 18-month prison sentence after he had stabbed the skipper of his boat (1993a). Yet another story stated that the number of women admitted to the crisis center in Reykjavík because of domestic violence had doubled in January 1993 compared with the levels in the previous year (1993c).

The total number of drug reports in 1993 was very similar to those cited in 1989. One drug story addressed a major drug bust at the Keflavík International Airport, where a Dutch citizen was arrested with 1.3 kilos of amphetamines (1993h). Apparently he had visited Iceland a total of 20 times in the previous three years, and it was stated that this was the largest seizure of amphetamines ever made at the Keflavík airport. Another news story covered a Supreme Court decision involving two males who were sentenced to four years in prison and fined for allegedly importing a total of 65 kilos of hashish in paint cans (1993g). Yet another report involved "20-year-old brothers sentenced to 12 months in prison" for selling a total of four kilos of hashish (1993b). Later, an editorial appeared, entitled "Drugs and Crime" (1993j), commenting on this two-pronged problem. Perhaps this spate of crime reporting was in part a consequence of an economic recession which plagued Iceland in the early 1990s, creating a feeling of general insecurity manifested by a deepening crime concern.

Three Decades of Icelandic Crime Reporting

To compensate for the lack of official data on crime, we reviewed the largest-circulation Icelandic newspaper for crime news. The total frequencies of types of crimes reported on in the press during the period 1969–1993 are found in the last column of table 4.1. There appeared an amazing consistency in the amount of crime news over the 20-year period from 1969 to 1989 with an average of approximately one crime news article for every day the newspaper was published. Then in 1993, we found a sharp increase in crime reporting for most types of crime. The total frequency ranged from a low of 229 in 1984 to a high of 409 in 1993. In Switzerland, Clinard (1978: 29) found two or three articles on crime per day in the average Swiss paper. Even though this represents a higher level of crime reporting in Switzerland than in Iceland, we must keep in mind the great population disparity between the two nations. Clinard reported that in the 1970s the population of Switzerland was 6.2 million (Clinard, 1978: 5), whereas Iceland had only about 265,000 inhabitants as late as 1995.

Another changing feature of crime reporting was the types of crime news articles. Reports of property crimes decreased sharply during this period, accounting for 65 percent of the total in 1969 but only 36 percent in 1979. In 1969 reports of property crimes not only constituted a greater proportion of the crime coverage but also tended to concentrate on relatively minor offenses. Inversely, during the three decades, reports of sex crimes, drug crimes, and crimes in the category "other violence" increased proportionately. Armed robberies first appeared in 1984. In 1969, drug reports were very rare, but that year the nation's first drug apprehension was reported to have taken place, and it generated considerable attention in the press. In the following years drug reporting became much more frequent and in 1979 accounted for nearly a quarter of all crime articles. Now these reports dealt with amphetamines and cocaine rather than merely cannabis, as had been the case in previous years. Yet throughout all these years cannabis-related stories continued to constitute the majority of all drug articles.

In 1974 there was a spate of articles on homicide, which corresponds with a peak of such cases reflected in the court statistics from the period. Sex-crime reporting ranged from a low of 4 percent of all crime stories in

1969 to a high of 10 percent in 1989. On the whole, crime was a frequent and constant topic in the paper but usually not prominently placed, nor was much space usually devoted to the subject. Crime reporting however became much more common in 1993, with more reports on property crimes, alcohol-related offenses such as illegal brewing, and sex and other violent crimes. For the first time, in 1993 there was an overall increased emphasis reflected in the number of crime-related articles. The press has predictably spread the alarm, just as official records have reflected increasing crime and disorder.

5
Fear of Crime in a Changing Society

"Three strikes and you're out" legislation in the United States seems driven by increasing punitiveness among the electorate. The courts are handing down ever harsher sentences, especially for drug offenders. Crime has become a dominant public issue in recent years even while crime rates have been falling. The media play a part in stoking the fires of fear and misperception of crime (McLeod et al., 1996). Also, public opinion has been whipped up to boost political careers. The Bush campaign in the 1988 presidential election used television commercials that drew on white racism legitimated by white fear of crime. The commercial featured a middle-class, white couple emotionally recounting the kidnapping, torture, humiliation, and rape experienced at the hands of a black male named Willie Horton (who was often pictured with a menacing scowl). He was a convicted murderer who had been furloughed from prison in Massachusetts by Governor Michael Dukakis, the Democratic presidential candidate (Galliher, 1991). After the commercial aired, George Bush surged in the polls, scoring special gains among white voters. This episode shows that media exposure of crime seems to have had an impact on citizens' perceptions of the crime problem, fueled as these sometimes are by white racism. While there are almost no racial minorities in Iceland, we will show that in this relatively egalitarian society, a deepened crime concern has nevertheless developed, possibly being fueled by increased media reporting of crime in recent years.

Attitude surveys have become more frequent in Iceland in the past few years. These surveys have covered a wide range of issues, including attitudes toward political parties, the mass media, and proposed legislation. These surveys have often been conducted by the social science faculty at the University of Iceland, in cooperation with the university's Social Science Research Institute (SSRI) (see, for example, Jónsson and Ólafsson, 1991). A general population survey of crime victimization and attitudes toward

61

crime had never been conducted in Iceland prior to 1989. The rudimentary status of official crime data in Iceland makes a survey of this kind especially useful.

We designed a set of questions addressing various issues relating to crime and, in cooperation with the SSRI, conducted two crime surveys. The first was in June of 1989. The interview schedule consisted of 10 items, covering a broad range of issues related to crime in Iceland. Among the issues raised in the survey were whether respondents believed crime in Iceland to be a serious problem, what their attitudes were toward criminal punishment, which type of crime they believed to be the most serious problem, what they believed to be the causes of crime, what their sense of security was, including whether they felt safe walking alone in their residential areas late at night, and finally, whether respondents had been victims of any crime in the last six months. The second survey took place in May of 1994 and was similar to the 1989 survey, allowing for comparisons between the samples. The findings of the surveys also enabled us to compare them with Clinard's and Balvig's observations of crime perceptions in Europe, discussed in chapter 1. Just as press reporting of crime-related news has dramatically increased in recent years, so does public opinion in Iceland reflect the gravity of the situation.

Personal Attitudes

The first survey used a random sample of 1,000 individuals from the national register, all between 15 and 80 years old. The response rate was approximately 73 percent, and a satisfactory congruence between the sample and the nation by sex, age, and location of residence was achieved. It is therefore reasoned that the sample adequately reflected the adult population as a whole. This survey used phone interviews by trained interviewers during a four-day period in June of 1989. The second survey, conducted in early May of 1994, involved a random sample of 1,500 individuals between the ages of 18 and 75. Again a satisfactory congruence between the sample and the nation was achieved, with a net response of approximately 74 percent.

The overwhelming majority believed crime to be a growing problem in 1989, as seen in table 5.1. Indeed, if available official data on crime are analyzed, an increase in crime can be detected between 1986 and 1988 (Kristmundsson, 1989: 11). During the time period 1974–1989 the number of criminal convictions increased sharply. In 1974 the number of criminal convictions was approximately 200, but it increased to 600 to 700 a year between 1986 and 1988. This finding seems to explain the perception of crime as a growing problem in Iceland, shown in the survey results. If we

Table 5.1. Do you believe crime to be a growing problem in Iceland? Percentage distribution of 1989 survey respondents, in total and by gender

	Yes	No
Total	90	10
Male	86	14
Female	95	5

analyze data provided by the director of public prosecutions regarding the number of indicted persons, a similar picture emerges. The number of indicted persons increased from 435 in 1980 (181.2 indictments per 100,000 persons) to 743 in 1989 (291.4 per 100,000). These criminal justice statistics all seem consistent with the survey data showing that crime is seen as an increasing problem.

Graphs 5.1, 5.2, and 5.3 display responses to a survey question regarding the overall severity of the crime problem. Over two-thirds of the total respondents in 1989 fell into the two categories of belief that crime is "somewhat great" or a "great problem" in Iceland, with more females than males responding one of these two ways (graph 5.1). Yet, within this mix, only a few believed crime to be a great problem, with more than half of all the respondents believing crime to be only somewhat of a problem. Perhaps the more interesting finding is that in 1989 nearly one-third of all respondents believed crime was not a major problem in Iceland, and only 12 percent believed it was. This does not come as a big surprise when we keep in mind that armed robbery has been extremely rare in Iceland, and intentional murder has been relatively infrequent compared with the rates of most other industrial nations (Archer and Gartner, 1984: 173ff.; Interpol, 1993). However, by 1994 these figures had reversed themselves. One-third of all respondents believed crime to be a great problem, and only 12 percent believed it to be minor. On what grounds respondents based their observations is open to speculation, but there is some evidence that, in general, crime survey respondents tend to base their views on mass media exposure rather than personal experience (Ericson et al., 1989; McLeod et al., 1996).

If we look at the age distribution of responses, it can be observed that there is a marked difference in the responses in the three age groups shown in graph 5.2. Respondents in the youngest age category were the least concerned with the threat of crime, and those in the oldest category were most concerned. Undoubtedly some of this difference may be a consequence of older Icelander's memories of life in Iceland when crime was

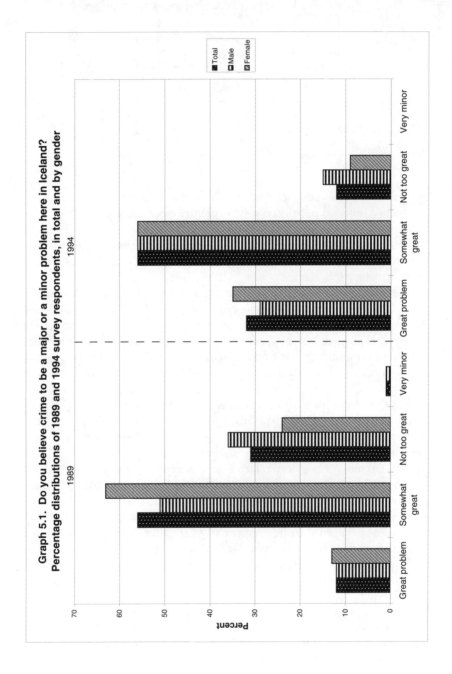

Graph 5.1. Do you believe crime to be a major or a minor problem here in Iceland? Percentage distributions of 1989 and 1994 survey respondents, in total and by gender

64

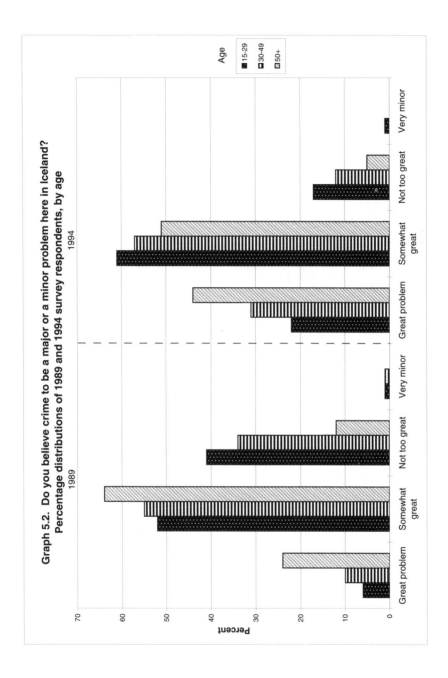

Graph 5.2. Do you believe crime to be a major or a minor problem here in Iceland? Percentage distributions of 1989 and 1994 survey respondents, by age

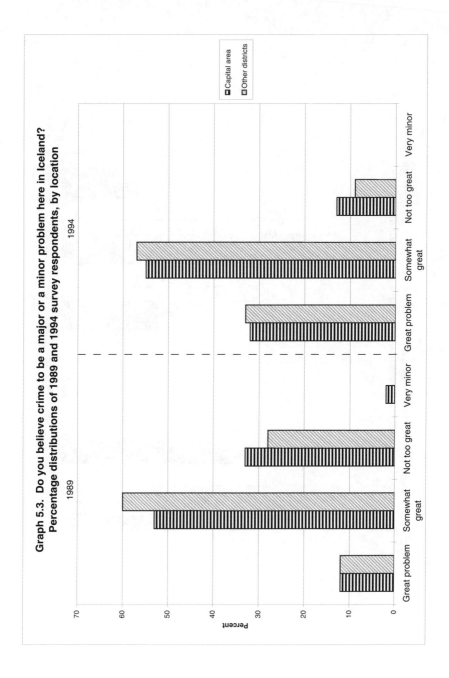

Graph 5.3. Do you believe crime to be a major or a minor problem here in Iceland? Percentage distributions of 1989 and 1994 survey respondents, by location

believed to be nearly nonexistent. The age difference holds in both surveys, with older respondents, like females, leaning more toward the position that the crime problem is of great significance. More of those respondents in the capital area believed crime to be a greater problem than those in rural areas (graph 5.3).

As can be seen in graphs 5.4 and 5.5, the findings in 1989 point in a definite direction: approximately three out of four respondents thought that punishment is too lenient in Iceland. Only a few believed punishments too harsh, while approximately 25 percent believed them to be reasonable. This finding might be partly explained by media reporting of sex crimes in Iceland, where, with the publication of the Rape Report (1989) just prior to the 1989 survey, the criminal justice system was put under critical scrutiny for being lenient and inefficient in handling sex offenses. Moreover, graph 5.4 indirectly indicates that most respondents also believed punishment for drug violations to be too lenient, since, as will be shown below, drug use was believed by the majority to be the most serious type of crime. This belief that penalties in Iceland are too lenient fits closely with the position taken by authorities, who earlier had adopted stiffer measures for drug violations, up to a maximum of 10 years in prison. When the findings are analyzed by age and gender groupings, it is apparent that all groups felt punishments are too lenient in Iceland. The findings of the 1994 survey reaffirm the position taken by respondents in 1989: most felt that punishments are too lenient. If anything this seems to be an increasing feeling, with more than 70 percent in 1989 believing punishments to be too lenient, and more than 80 percent in 1994 believing so. Surveys in other countries show a similar tendency. This is true even in the United States, where very severe penalties have been adopted (Roberts and Stalans, 1997).

It is evident from graph 5.6 that many believed drug use to be the most serious crime problem facing Icelanders, 40 percent of respondents in 1989 and nearly one-third in 1994. Over 20 percent thought that sex offenses were the most serious problem in both 1989 and 1994, with more females than males agreeing in both surveys. The most remarkable change in perception concerns violence other than sex crimes. Only 14 percent believed other violent crimes to be the most serious form of crime in 1989, with this number rising to 30 percent in 1994. Another noteworthy change concerns burglary, which in 1994 was believed by 10 percent to be the most serious crime, up from 4 percent in 1989. This view fits closely with the increase in burglaries reported to police in recent years.

The survey finding of great public anxiety about drugs reflects the concerns of local authorities. Icelandic authorities have taken unusual steps to curb this problem by establishing a separate drug police and a drug court.

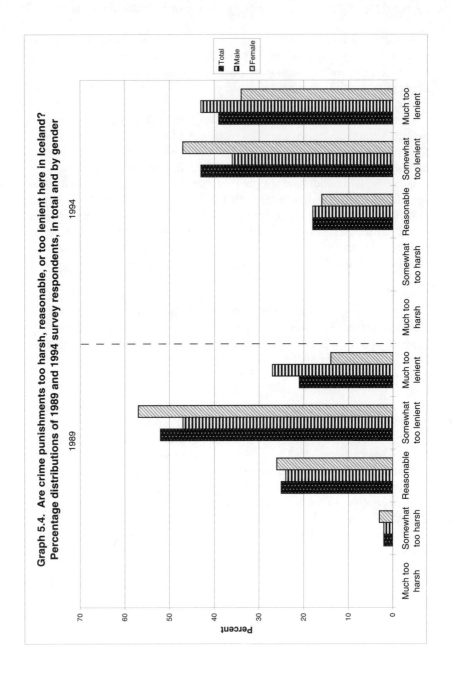

Graph 5.4. Are crime punishments too harsh, reasonable, or too lenient here in Iceland?
Percentage distributions of 1989 and 1994 survey respondents, in total and by gender

68

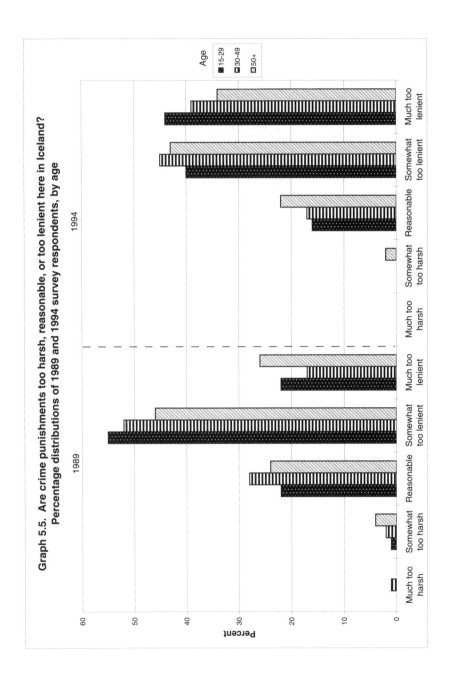

Graph 5.5. Are crime punishments too harsh, reasonable, or too lenient here in Iceland?
Percentage distributions of 1989 and 1994 survey respondents, by age

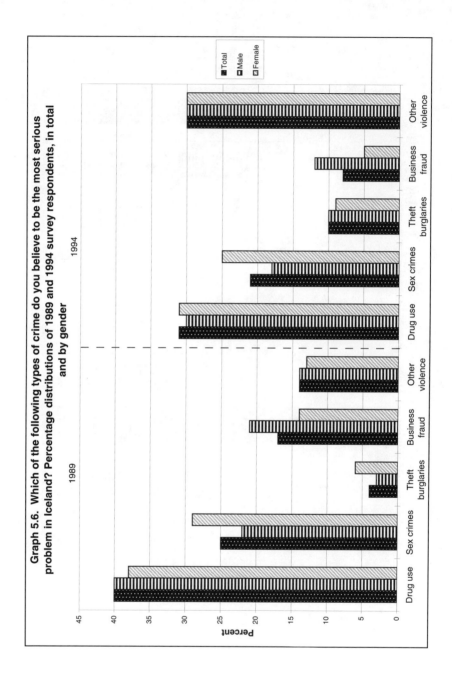

Graph 5.6. Which of the following types of crime do you believe to be the most serious problem in Iceland? Percentage distributions of 1989 and 1994 survey respondents, in total and by gender

70

As for sex crimes, this issue created such great concern that Parliament passed a resolution in 1984 calling for an evaluation of how sex crimes were handled by the criminal justice system. This report was finally introduced to the public in the year prior to our first survey (although it was formally published in 1989), and it received wide media attention. Predictably, concern about this subject is also reflected in our survey results.

As graph 5.7 demonstrates, age does not change the general picture of perceptions of the most serious crimes, but there are some differences. Younger respondents tended on both occasions to downplay the significance of drug offenses and emphasized more the seriousness of sex crimes and other violence. Older respondents emphasized drug offenses. The most likely explanation for these differences is that they are a result of the personal experiences of these people. Surveys of drug use in Iceland, such as that by Gunnlaugsson (1998), have shown that use of illegal drugs occurs almost solely among the young. Their personal experience with these substances apparently makes these people less fearful about them in general.

Looking at graphs 5.8 and 5.9, we can see that the position of respondents on this question of the causes of crime is clear and has apparently not changed over this five-year period. More than half of the respondents believed either alcohol or drug abuse to be the main reason for criminality, and more than one-fifth believed it to be a result of a difficult home life. Approximately 16 percent believed it to be a result of bad associations. These explanations seem to have certain shared assumptions. More than 90 percent of the respondents in both years believed the most important explanation for crime in Iceland to be various social-psychological factors in the life of offenders, such as substance abuse, broken homes, and bad associations. Economic conditions are not widely seen as producing crime in Iceland. Moreover, very few believed lenient penalties to be responsible for crime, which suggests that even though the majority indicated that penalties are too lenient in Iceland, this is not such an extreme problem that it is blamed for the genesis of criminal behavior.

These findings seem to fit closely with the position taken by several representatives of the criminal justice system. Our interviews with leading personnel in the Justice Ministry, the State Criminal Investigative Police, prison guards, and even inmates revealed that substance abuse and broken homes are characteristic of repeat offenders and are seen as the most important factors leading to crime. Poverty and insufficient opportunity do not appear as major explanations for crime. Thus, it is not the changing social structure which is believed to lead to crime in Iceland, but rather personal misfortune or failure. Social structural theories, which address the linkage of social class and crime, do not seem to have much support

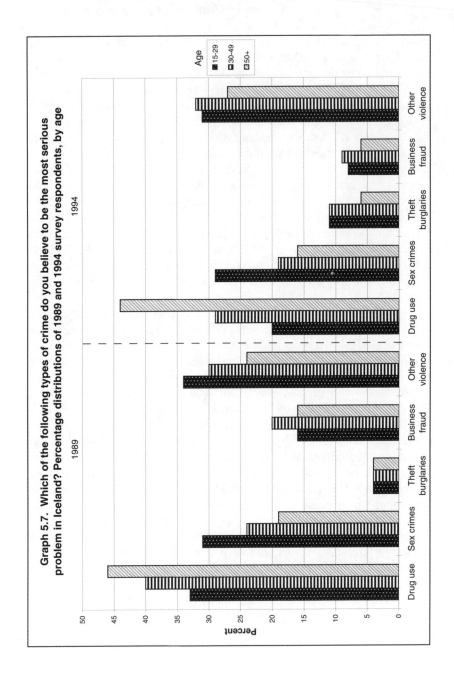

Graph 5.7. Which of the following types of crime do you believe to be the most serious problem in Iceland? Percentage distributions of 1989 and 1994 survey respondents, by age

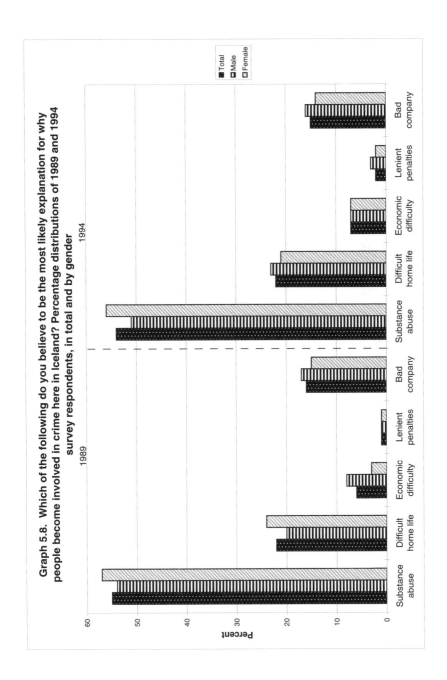

Graph 5.8. Which of the following do you believe to be the most likely explanation for why people become involved in crime here in Iceland? Percentage distributions of 1989 and 1994 survey respondents, in total and by gender

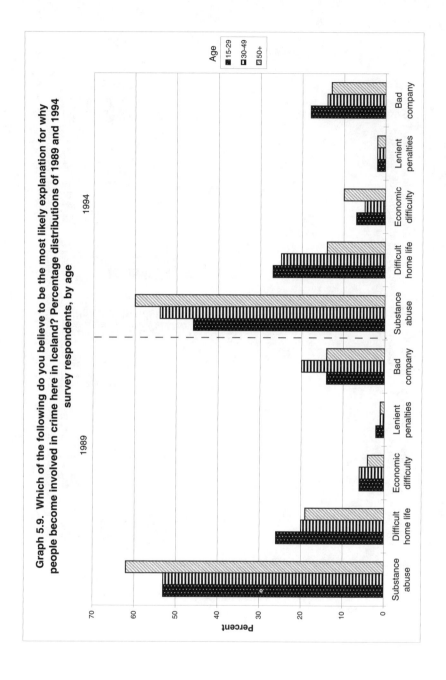

Graph 5.9. Which of the following do you believe to be the most likely explanation for why people become involved in crime here in Iceland? Percentage distributions of 1989 and 1994 survey respondents, by age

among citizens or the authorities, possibly because social stratification has not been believed to be extensive in Iceland.

In graphs 5.10 and 5.11 the position of respondents is clear, for the group as a whole, for males and females, and for all age groups. The overwhelming majority (87 percent in both 1989 and 1994, as shown in graph 5.10) opposed the idea of the death penalty. The idea of capital punishment seemed to be an alien phenomenon to most respondents and perhaps manifests itself most clearly in the position of Iceland's former president Vigdís Finnbogadóttir. Before the presidential elections in 1988, she was forthright in her opposition to the idea of capital punishment. In a local televised news report she was asked if she would ever think of opposing legislation passed by Parliament. She claimed that to be unlikely but added that if Parliament would take the extreme action of passing a law allowing capital punishment, she would veto it. The death penalty was abolished in 1928, but prior to that no executions had taken place for almost a century (since 1830).

Victimization and Fear of Crime

Respondents were asked in 1989 and 1994 about their personal experiences with crime victimization. In 1989 they were asked about their victimization during the past six months and in 1994 during the past year. Fourteen percent in 1989 indicated that they or someone in their family had been a crime victim during the past six months, and 21 percent in 1994 said that they had been victimized during the past year. All this shows that Iceland is not a crime-free paradise, even though there may be less crime victimization than in other countries.

Table 5.2 indicates that of those who had been victimized in 1989, one-half had experienced property damage to their home or automobile. A little over one-third had been victimized by theft or robbery, and little over one-fourth by a business fraud. Of those who had been victimized in 1994, about half had been victims of theft or a burglary, and about two-fifths had experienced vandalism. Just over half of those victimized in both years had reported the crime to the police—55 percent in 1989 and 57 percent in 1994.

Victimization surveys, which have been conducted frequently in the United States, have routinely shown that official statistics of crime, such as police or court data, underestimate the amount of crime in society (Siegel, 1995: 57). A large portion of criminal victimizations are never reported to the police, creating what has been called the dark figure of crime. For example, comparisons between the *National Crime Survey* (NCS) and the *Uniform Crime Report* (UCR) reveal that reports of crime victimizations

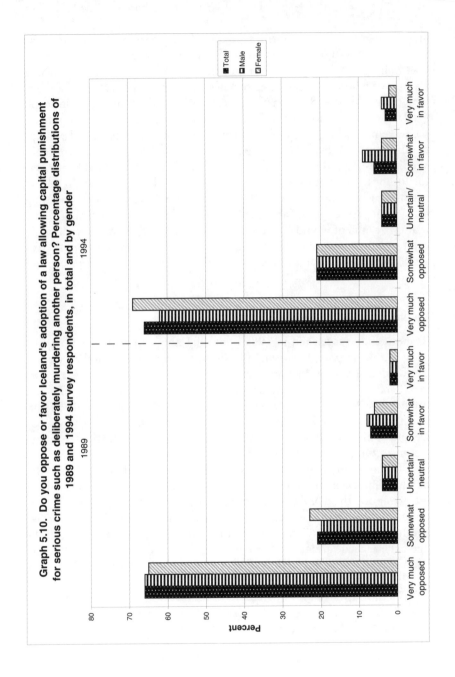

Graph 5.10. Do you oppose or favor Iceland's adoption of a law allowing capital punishment for serious crime such as deliberately murdering another person? Percentage distributions of 1989 and 1994 survey respondents, in total and by gender

76

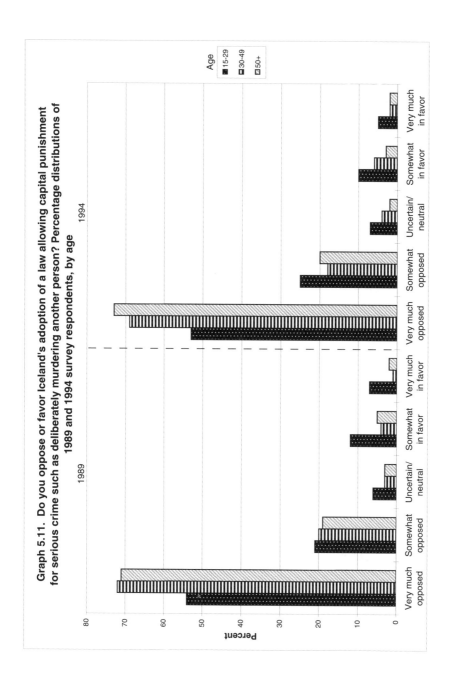

Graph 5.11. Do you oppose or favor Iceland's adoption of a law allowing capital punishment for serious crime such as deliberately murdering another person? Percentage distributions of 1989 and 1994 survey respondents, by age

Table 5.2. Have you, or has anyone in your family, been a victim of any of the
following crimes in the past six months (or the past year)? Percentage
distribution of 1989 and 1994 survey respondents, by type of crime
experienced, gender, and area of residence

	Assault	Theft/ robbery	Property damage	Sex crime	Business fraud	Other
			1989[a]			
Yes	2	5	7	0	4	0
No	98	95	93	100	96	100
Male	3	6	8	0	4	0
Female	2	4	5	0	4	0
Capital area	3	7	6	0	5	0
Other districts	1	2	7	0	3	0
			1994[b]			
Yes	4	10	9	1	5	0
No	96	90	91	99	95	100
Male	5	11	11	0	7	0
Female	4	9	6	1	4	0
Capital area	4	12	9	1	5	0
Other districts	5	7	7	0	5	0

Note: Some respondents in both years reported crime victimization in more
than one category.
[a]The period in question in the 1989 survey was the past six months.
[b]The period in question in the 1994 survey was the past year.

were up to four times greater than the rate reported in the *UCR* for the
same year (McCaghy, 1985: 152).

It seems apparent that a gap exists, both in the United States and in
Iceland, between the amount of crime reported to police and the amount of
crime victimization. Moreover, on the basis of this survey, this gap seems
to be greater in the United States than in Iceland, with more than half of the
victimization in Iceland being reported to police, compared with more
than half of the victimization for most categories of crime going unreported to police in the United States (*Criminal Victimization in the United
States, 1986*, 1988: 10). Perhaps the small size of the population in Iceland
creates a feeling that the police can be more effective than they are believed

to be in the United States, with its heavily populated and heterogeneous society. Another likely explanation involves the general relationship between the police and the public. For some time studies have shown that in the United States there is a lack of confidence in the police expressed by large segments of the public (Boggs and Galliher, 1975), especially in the black community, where opposition to the police is legendary (Lasley, 1994; Parker et al., 1995). Similar research in Iceland shows much greater confidence and trust in the police (Jónsson and Ólafsson, 1991).

Table 5.3 shows that, in 1989 and 1994, most respondents felt safe walking alone late at night. This was especially true for males, of whom more than 80 percent claimed to feel safe compared with approximately 64 percent of females. This suggests that there did not seem to be a rampant crime scare among respondents. This finding is also analyzed by comparing the capital area with other districts. More than half of the nation's population of 270,000 lives in the urban capital area, with over 150,000 residents, compared with the next largest community of Akureyri, with only 15,000 residents. Those who reside in the capital area tended to feel

Table 5.3. Do you feel safe when walking alone late at night in your residential area? Percentage distributions of 1989 and 1994 survey respondents, by gender and area of residence

	Very unsafe	Somewhat unsafe	Somewhat safe	Very safe
1989				
Total respondents	11	14	31	44
Male	9	7	32	52
Female	13	23	29	35
Capital area	13	23	37	27
Other districts	8	3	22	67
1994				
Total respondents	11	16	33	40
Male	6	9	31	54
Female	14	23	35	28
Capital area	14	24	41	22
Other districts	6	7	24	63

Note: Rows may not add to 100% because of rounding.

less secure than those living in other districts; more than two-thirds of those living in other districts in 1989 felt very safe compared with approximately one-fourth of those living in the capital area. More than one-third felt unsafe in the capital area in 1989, while just over 10 percent felt unsafe in other districts. While crime in the streets of the capital area has repeatedly been reported in the media in recent years, it seems not to have produced a sense of great fear among most of the public, even in Reykjavík. Thus, the findings in 1994 are not markedly different from those in 1989. Even though respondents believed crime to be a greater problem in 1994 than in 1989, this has not yet had a major impact on personal perceptions of security.

Increasing Fear of Increasing Crime

To gain a more direct measure of public perceptions of the crime problem in Iceland, we conducted a national survey of opinion and experience in 1989 and in 1994. In 1989, more than two-thirds of the respondents in this survey believed crime to be a significant problem, and more than 90 percent believed that its dimensions are growing. In 1994 the concern had deepened, with about one-third believing crime is a very great problem compared with 12 percent in that category in 1989. Approximately three-fourths believed punishments in the country to be too lenient in 1989, going up to about 80 percent in 1994. Drug use was widely believed to be the most serious type of crime in the nation in 1989 and 1994. More than half in both 1989 and 1994 believed that substance abuse is what leads people into crime. Thus, in these ways public opinion was consistent with press-reporting practices. In 1997, we conducted a third survey. At that time, 43 percent felt that crime was a very great problem, compared with 32 percent in 1994 and 12 percent in 1989. As for the problem of drugs, 50 percent felt that they were the most serious problem in 1997, compared with 40 percent in 1989 and 31 percent in 1994. The results of these surveys further demonstrate the ever-deepening concern with crime and drugs.

6

Sex Laws and Sex Crimes
in a Land of Equals

Some argue that unsubstantiated charges of rape can result in ruined reputations. Many rapes involve two people where there are no witnesses and no conclusive physical evidence, which accounts for the frequent difficulty in prosecuting such cases. Moreover, traditionally, rape by a stranger has been handled by law enforcement authorities with much greater concern than rape allegations against someone known by the victim (Estrich, 1987). The clear implication is that if a victim knows her assailant, then perhaps any alleged sexual contact is not really rape. In very small, homogeneous societies one might imagine that this could pose an especially vexing problem. In this chapter, the question is, How are rape charges typically played out in Iceland? We examine the social reality of sex crimes in Iceland, especially in view of a government report on this issue in 1989 and its impact on the handling of rape charges in the criminal justice system. Moreover, we evaluate the report's suggestions for legal reform, as well as the social policy recommended for the treatment of sex offenders. In the chapters that follow the contradictions between the prosecutions of rape and drug offenses will become readily apparent.

The Icelandic Rape Report

Encouraged by the Women's Alliance Party, in 1984 the Icelandic parliament, in an unprecedented move, passed the following resolution: "Parliament instructs the minister of justice to appoint a five person committee to evaluate police investigations and legal proceedings in rape cases and propose reforms in this subject matter" (Parliamentary Debates, 1983–1984b: 4961–4962). This move by Parliament was unusual, because rarely had the subject of crime been put on the Parliament's agenda as a pressing issue, except for discussions of alcohol and drugs. What triggered this move by Parliament was a case in Reykjavík where the alleged offender had been arrested for two rapes, taken into custody, and then released after a preliminary police investigation (see "Crime Reports in 1984" in chapter 4). This event created considerable media attention, and questions about how these issues were handled by local authorities were widely discussed, leading to the action by Parliament. During the parliamentary debate on this issue, the sponsor of the resolution noted:

> We do not believe that the penal code needs to be changed. Yet, it is evident that almost never are the stiffest dimensions of penal sentencing options being handed out by the courts . . . with penalties usually being twelve to eighteen months in prison for rape. . . . Everyone who I have spoken to in preparation of this resolution fully agrees that conditions of victims in rape cases are in many ways unique and worse than for victims of other offenses. The objective of the resolution is to improve this situation. (Parliamentary Debates, 1983–1984b: 4962, 4965)

The resolution was consequently passed with no opposition votes. This concern was shared by many Icelanders. The public attitude survey of 1989, discussed earlier, revealed that one-fourth of all respondents believed sex offenses to be the most serious type of crime in Iceland. In 1989, the committee (a criminologist, a physician and member of Parliament, a social worker, and two attorneys) that had been appointed by the minister of justice finally issued its report on rape in Iceland.

Sex Crimes and the Law in Early Iceland

Rape has been known in Iceland from the beginning of its settlement and has traditionally carried stiff penalties. Iceland's first law book (Grágás), which was in effect for more than two centuries (well into the thirteenth century), had an article indicating total exile of an offender who had forced a woman into sexual intercourse. Exile at this early time in this hostile climate meant certain death in many cases. In 1281, Iceland's parliament passed a new law (Jónsbók), which adopted a stiffer penalty for rape: the offender could now be executed, but at the same time, the offender could under some circumstances pay a fine to the Church and then be exempted from punishment (Ingvarsson, 1970). Under Jónsbók, iron branding was also allowed (Sæmundsson, 1990). In 1564, another law was passed (Stóri Dómur), which was even stiffer; now there was unconditional execution for sex crimes; males were beheaded for committing such crimes, and females were drowned for such crimes committed against them. Yet Icelanders were reluctant to enforce this law, which nonetheless stayed in effect well into the nineteenth century. Even though death was mandatory, the Danish king received considerable sums of money during this period from offenders paying fines to save themselves from execution (Rape Report, 1989). In Iceland's penal code of 1869, rape was still described as a very serious crime, but now the character of the victim could also be considered. The offense was not considered as serious if the victim had a bad reputation.

We will examine three infamous Icelandic rape cases from centuries past to help shed some light on the current problems of enforcement (Helgason, 1960, 1980). In 1504 a man was convicted of raping a woman and was punished by losing the fingers of his left hand. This punishment was reportedly lighter than usual because the victim did not report the crime to the authorities as required by law but only confided the offense to two young female relatives (Helgason, 1980: 21). In 1543 a German sea-man from a merchant vessel was convicted of rape and sanctioned by los-ing either one or two fingers. If he could swear under an oath that he had not committed the crime he would lose only one finger, but he would lose both if he failed in performing the oath. Moreover, if he failed to perform the oath, he could still have been punished with execution if he was not granted the "mercy of the King." This procedure, involving mercy from the (Danish) king, was an integral part of Iceland's legal system at the time (Helgason, 1980: 137). This practice was in effect for centuries under the Danish colonial system, and today there is still a sign of it: Iceland's presi-dent is authorized according to the constitution to exempt offenders from conviction (Article 29). In the 1543 case the offender ultimately was able to pay a fine to the king to save his fingers and also pay a fee to the victim as compensation. As these cases illustrate, corporal punishment was a com-mon legal practice into the sixteenth century, and flogging and branding remained a part of the law for a long period after that. Flogging, for exam-ple, as punishment for rape was practiced into the nineteenth century (Rape Report, 1989).

In the third case, in 1725, a farmer was beheaded at Þingvellir, his corpse was burned, and his head was put on a pole for raping his 20-year-old daughter and for burying their offspring (Helgason, 1960: 82). It is interesting to note that even though the daughter did not know what had happened to the child, since her father had taken it away immediately after its delivery, she was sentenced as well, to drowning, for having a child as a result of an illicit sexual union (although her case was forwarded to the Danish king for possible mercy). Thus, sex crimes carried stiff penalties and were enforced at Þingvellir, where the old Icelandic parliament met into the early nineteenth century. Offenders were believed to be responsi-ble for their acts, and it was assumed that they could choose not to commit the crime. At the time there was not much differentiation between secular and Church powers, for the judge and the clergy gradually formed an alliance in the seventeenth century in carrying out convictions and enforcing the law (see, e.g., Sæmundsson, 1990), with the Church gradually losing power to the state from the eighteenth century onward.

Contradictions in the Development of Rape Law in Iceland

The penal code enacted in 1869 remained in effect until new legislation was passed in 1940. The new code stated that if a female was forced into sexual intercourse by violence or threats of violence, a defendant could be punished by imprisonment for not less than 1 year up to 16 years maximum, or a life sentence in extreme cases. These sentences were high by Icelandic standards in providing both a high minimum and high maximum. This held also for rape attempts, but in such cases there was an option of reducing the sentence. This was similar to the range of punishments for homicide, which has been from five years to life imprisonment.

In 1979, a total of nine offenders were serving terms in prison for sex crimes, and in 1996 this number rose to 34, the highest number in recent history. However, although more persons served time in prison for various sex crimes during the last decades of the century than had earlier, the average period of time actually served in prison for different forms of crime decreased in the 1980s (Kristmundsson, 1989: 45). In recent years the most common punishment for rape has been imprisonment for 12 to 18 months. If the offender is convicted of two rapes or more, the sentence is usually longer: four years in prison. The harshest rape sentence under the 1940 law was given in 1961: a 10-year prison sentence. The reason for this relatively stiff sentence was that this incident involved an especially brutal assault (Rape Report, 1989: 121–122).

At least in a formal sense penalties for rape are relatively severe. A minimum prison sentence in the penal code is stipulated only for rape and intentional homicide; for other offenses only a maximum prison sentence is specified. In general, however, the actual sentencing in rape cases seems to be closer to the minimum. In addition, many believe that much rape goes unreported and therefore never reaches the courts. This situation can be compared with that of the United Kingdom, for example, where 78 percent of all rapes are believed to be unreported to the police (Rape Report, 1989: 352). In the United States only about half of all rapes are reported to police (Siegel, 1995: 299). Another source in the United States indicates that unreported rape may even be higher (Russell, 1985).

Research on the reporting rate of rapes has not yet been conducted in Iceland, but in the Rape Report there is an overview of all rapes reported to the State Criminal Investigative Police (SCIP) from 1 July 1977 (when SCIP was founded), through 31 December 1983. During this time period a total of 126 cases were reported to the SCIP involving a sexual assault on a female (Rape Report, 1989: 153), which equates to police handling about 20 such cases a year during this time period, or a rate of 8.6 offenses per 100,000 people. According to the Rape Report, this rate of rape is similar to those of most other Scandinavian countries. The questions which come to mind are, How many of these cases known to police were actually prosecuted? and How many ended in conviction of the offender? If the legal fate of these 126 cases is analyzed (Rape Report, 1989: 160), it appears that 42 of them simply ended at the SCIP. The SCIP did not see grounds for forwarding the cases to the prosecutor because the victims wanted to drop the charges. The remaining 84 cases were forwarded to the director of public prosecutions (DPP), and of these, 48 were formally charged and sent to court. The DPP dropped the charges in the 36 remaining cases. Of these 48 cases forwarded to court, 38 ended in conviction of the offender, 2 ended in acquittals, and 6 were unresolved at the time of the report. Of these 38 convictions, 30 were for rape, and the others involved lesser charges.

Thus, it appears that only about one-third of the rape cases reported to SCIP actually ended with conviction of the offender; one-third ended with the SCIP, and an additional one-third were dropped by the prosecutor. This reluctance of the criminal justice system to actually convict for an alleged sex crime is unusual when compared with other serious crimes. In chapter 7 we note that only 1 percent of drug cases ended in acquittal during the 1980s. In the time period 1979–1986, most cases of homicide and manslaughter ended in conviction, as did about two-thirds of all crimes of violence. It appears that the figure for all sex offenses continued in the 1980s to be approximately one-third of all cases known to SCIP (Kristmundsson, 1989: 35).

For a conviction the legal system usually requires more than the sole accusation made by the victim, in order to prevent the conviction of an innocent person on the basis of false testimony. The prosecution is required to prove the criminal intent of the offender. This is difficult, since a common response of rapists is that they did not intend to rape, or that the act took place with the consent of the victim, or at least that was what they believed (Rape Report, 1989). The victim's side of the story may become almost irrelevant if the prerequisite for rape is that the offender actually intended to rape. The court, therefore, also seeks other evidence beyond the testimony of those involved in order to demonstrate criminal intent of rape. This is often found in bodily bruises, ripped clothing, signs of blood on victims, or signs of violence in the place where the incident occurred. If nothing of this sort can be detected, it seems very unlikely that such a case will end in conviction, but the probability is that the crime is unlikely to be reported to police in the first place, even when victims believe they have been raped.

Of the 126 cases of rape known to the police during 1977–1983 and reviewed in the Rape Report, cases ending in conviction show much more violence than cases being dropped, the people involved knew each other personally in few cases, and the victims showed much greater signs of resistance and had more bruises than victims in other cases (Rape Report, 1989: 186). If characteristics of offenders are analyzed in cases ending in conviction, the culprits tend to be younger than the alleged offenders in dropped cases, are repeat offenders, and were intoxicated while committing their crime. The victims in cases ending in conviction also tend to be younger, but were usually not intoxicated and have fewer previous criminal records than victims in cases that were dropped (Rape Report, 1989: 167–170). It is, therefore, obvious that many variables, including offender and victim characteristics, affect the legal outcome. It is not surprising, given these conditions, that there is often an unwillingness among female victims of rape to report the crime to the police. It seems that the picture that agencies of the criminal justice system have of rape is that of a sex-crazed stranger violently attacking a young virgin who resists in vain and is eventually overwhelmed by her attacker. Cases falling outside these conditions have difficulty in the criminal justice system, in Iceland and elsewhere (Estrich, 1987).

However, explanations for the nature of the legal processing of rape cases involve more than police and court procedures. Many feminist scholars (see, for example, Russell, 1985; and Mackinnon, 1989) contend that rape can be adequately understood only in terms of dominant notions of masculinity and femininity. Sexual aggression, even violent assault, represents qualities viewed by many as being masculine, demonstrating strength and independence. Feminine qualities, on the other hand, reflect the opposite: weakness, passivity, and submissiveness. Thus, as Diane Russell has pointed out, much rape is not so much a deviant act as it is an overconforming act, an exaggerated form of "normal" relations existing between the sexes (Russell, 1985: 260). In this respect, as the Rape Report noted, many accused rapists claimed that they had not intended to rape but had simply intended to have sexual intercourse and furthermore believed that the woman had consented even though she resisted (Rape Report, 1989: 109–110).

Yet, in the world of legal justice, the mission is to find the guilt or innocence, and this cannot be multifaceted or contradictory; it must be unified. If the female victim believes she was raped and the male claims he simply intended to have sexual intercourse, the justice system confronts a contradictory case. The world of legal justice is, in fact, mostly defined by men (Estrich, 1987: 65). The female victim more often than not seems to lose out; her side of the story becomes suspicious, and the man's side of the story tends more often to become defined as reality. Just as criminologists sometimes speak of "victimless crimes," referring to crimes such as drug use and prostitution, rape cases seem to represent a new category of "crimes without an offender" (Bjarnason, 1990). In victimless crimes, all those taking part in the act are believed to be perpetrators, not victims. For instance, even though drug pushers benefit at the expense of drug users, pushers still view themselves as allies of users. The police need to be able to substantiate a transaction of this kind of crime to prove it later in court, because what is needed for conviction is not proof that the drug pusher intended to destroy another person's life or health but simply a demonstration that a drug transaction took place. Notice how different the legal reasoning is for rape. In rape cases the female victim's side of the story tends to be rejected if a defendant asserts that he intended not to rape but merely to engage in sexual intercourse. The woman appears to the police, prosecutors, and the courts to be a victim of a crime where there is no offender (see also Estrich, 1987). And a crime without an offender does not exist in criminal law.

Recall that Gusfield has distinguished between symbolic and instrumental properties of law (Gusfield, 1963). Laws serve a symbolic function merely by affirming the superiority of one set of norms over another; they do not rely on actual enforcement to have an impact. In his study of American prohibition of alcohol, Gusfield shows evidence of the symbolic role of law, in that prohibition was widely violated yet seldom enforced. A major role of this law was, according to Gusfield, to bolster the self-esteem of the middle-class, rural Protestants who pressed for the law's passage and who felt reassured, even if the law was enforced only sporadically. Rape laws appear to have a similar symbolic quality: they are firm and decisive on the face of it, symbolically reassuring superior morals and promising protection, but they are only sporadically enforced.

Continuing Contradictions in Policy Recommendations

A part of the role of the committee appointed by Parliament in 1984 was to recommend reforms in the justice system in regard to the legal processing of sex crimes. Even though the problems of rape cases discussed above were not solved, the committee did consider various remedies believed to be necessary and significant. Among the resolutions the committee suggested was the opening of a crisis center for victims of sex crimes and other violent assaults; the center was to operate in close association with police and medical personnel. Second, the committee suggested that the law be changed to exclude one's gender from consideration, for the existing law allowed only the rape of women. Third, the committee recommended changing the definition of what constitutes rape so that the occurrence of actual sexual intercourse is no longer required for the act to qualify as rape; rather, the definition would be broadened to encompass other sexually related acts. Furthermore, the Rape Report recommended that as much as possible the previous sexual history of victims be excluded from consideration. Also, the committee recommended that the prosecutor be obliged to state openly the reasons that a case was being dropped. Finally, the committee suggested that the state should be made accountable for failed payments of compensation to victims by offenders.

Most of the legal reforms suggested were put into the law passed in 1992; victims' gender was excluded from the law and the definition of what constitutes rape was broadened. Under the revised code a rape could involve other unspecified acts aside from intercourse, which would be determined at the discretion of the judge. The new law in regard to rape (Article 194) now reads as follows:

> Those who force a person by violence or threat of violence to sexual intercourse or other sexually related acts are punishable by imprisonment for not less than a year or up to a 16 year maximum. What constitutes violence is denial of personal liberty by confining or by use of drugs or other related actions.

The legal changes just described could possibly improve the situation of victims and perhaps decrease the number of unreported rapes in Iceland. However, even if incidents are reported at a higher rate, the question remains whether the rate of dropped cases will decrease, especially keeping in mind the prerequisite in the law that the offender actually intended to rape. As long as stringent "criminal intent" is maintained in the law, it is difficult to envision a dramatic change in convictions or an increased reporting of rape, even though the definition of rape has been broadened. The Icelandic penal law states in regard to criminal intent:

> Criminal intent . . . may be lacking, if the perpetrator has not taken resistance seriously, because of reasonable grounds such as previous acquaintance [of the victim] or because he did not realize that he caused fear of harm in the mind of [the victim]. . . . If the perpetrator has a reason to believe that there is consent, his behavior is not punishable. (Article 18, 1988)

Despite the present law in rape cases that stipulates a minimum of 1 year in prison all the way up to a maximum of 16 years incarceration,

Article 15 (1988) in the penal law states: "Those persons shall not be punished who because of insanity, mental retardation or decay, state of limited consciousness, were unable at the time of committing their crime to control their behavior." The conflict involved in these two assumptions about offenders, expressed in the paragraphs above—one stipulating punishment based on a free choice and criminal intent; the other, an exemption from punishment due to psychological factors—has become increasingly apparent in recent years. A prison sentence rests on the assumption that offenders freely choose to commit their crimes and that they are responsible for the crimes. Such persons are punished with a prison sentence to deter them and others from engaging in crime in the future. The second assumption, however, rests on an entirely different principle. There, offenders are viewed as not being responsible for their crimes, and, therefore, punishment of them is believed to be unjustifiable. Instead, the notion of treatment, either psychological or medical, is offered in place of punishment.

The reforms suggested by the committee in the Rape Report tended in part to play into the latter assumption, by stressing the therapeutic mission of the law at the expense of the punitive approach. This is manifested first in a lighter range of penalties recommended, from a minimum of 30 days in prison up to a maximum of 10 years. If, however, the act involved the use of a knife or a gun, the maximum prison sentence could be escalated to 16 years. In addition, it was suggested that rehabilitation of offenders should be considered as an alternative: "It is a pity how little is being done in providing assistance to rapists and their families" (Rape Report, 1989: 293). This view was supported by experience in other countries, which had shown rehabilitation to be possible:

> The vast majority of rapists being reviewed here have a long history of crime and are socially in a disadvantageous position. These facts support the necessity of exploring the possibility of rehabilitation. It has been demonstrated abroad that specific rehabilitative measures, such as social training, psycho-medical treatment, educational opportunity and vocational training have managed to alter earlier causal factors and to help develop more positive and stable self-images of violators. This effort might also change their attitude and strengthen their interactive abilities and decrease the likelihood of repeat offenses. (Rape Report, 1989: 79)

Moreover, it was suggested that the option be left open for the director of public prosecutions to drop formal charges if a violator appears not to be accountable for his act and to exempt a suspect from solitary confinement if it is felt to be unnecessary to segregate that suspect during the initial investigation (Rape Report, 1989). It is apparent that the proposals of reform provided by the rape committee tended in part to be located within a theoretical framework which implied that the offender is not believed to be totally responsible for his conduct and, therefore, should not be punished. If the conditions leading to his unlawful behavior are removed, conventional behavior becomes possible.

As has been pointed out by many observers (see Conrad and Schneider, 1992), in contemporary, technologically oriented welfare societies the management of deviance is increasingly placed in the hands of specialists, with deviance being conceptualized as evidence of "sickness" rather than "badness." These specialists include various professionals, such as psychiatrists and social scientists, who claim expertise on the subject and who increasingly share social-control decisions with the courts. This development in approaching deviance is not necessarily a result of any scientific achievements, but is a political process, a result of claims-making activity of various interest groups (Little, 1983; and Conrad and Schneider, 1992). Although this development is often promoted as being humanitarian and suited to meet individual needs, the end result is that responsibility of the individual for his own conduct becomes somewhat blurred and subject to debate and expert testimony. Moreover, the question of guilt or innocence becomes irrelevant, for now the focus is not on the criminal act but rather on the nature of the offender.

The Development of Rape Cases in Recent Years

The question remains, Has there been a marked change in the frequency of rape cases in the criminal justice system since the period 1977–1983, covered in the Rape Report? During the eight-year period from 1988 through 1995, the SCIP received 168 charges of rape, or 21 charges per year on the average. This represents a pattern very similar to that of the period from 1977 to 1983, when the annual average number of rape charges was 20. Even since the legal reform in 1992, the average number has been only slightly higher, with about 22 charges a year.

In addition to the reporting of rape, there is the issue of the processing of rape charges in the criminal justice system. During 1989–1992 prosecutors apparently dropped charges in a total of 48 rape cases (Parliamentary Files, 1993–1994: case no. 225). The primary reason given for dropping charges involved the belief that conviction was unlikely, which pertained to 22 of those cases. In 1992, not a single charge was dropped because of unlikely conviction. The legal change made in 1992, which involved broadening the definition of rape, might therefore have had some impact on the processing of such cases.

On the whole it might be argued, on the basis of the very early applications of the new law, that the legal change made in 1992 could have at least some impact on the processing of rape charges. Fewer cases have been dropped by the prosecutor since the passage of the law, possibly because of the broader definition of what constitutes rape. Yet, the legal reforms do not seem to have had an impact on rape reporting to the police. Victims apparently need more time to be convinced that these reforms are genuine. Moreover, broadening the definition of rape does not impact the issue of criminal intent, which still needs to be demonstrated. If criminal intent is missing, a new and broader definition of rape seems irrelevant.

Another perspective on this issue is reflected in the recent experience of the Crisis Center for Rape Victims (Neyðarmóttaka vegna nauðgunar), established in 1993 and located at the Reykjavík City Hospital. While the center has not published any reports, its records indicate 386 individuals sought its services from 1993 through 1998 (March 1999 interview with staff member). Most contacting the center had been victims of rape. Of these individuals, 210 (or 54 percent) reported the incident to the police. And of those cases reported to the police, 132 (63 percent) were forwarded to the director of public prosecutions. The prosecutors in turn indicted 64 cases (48 percent). Thus, of the 210 cases initially reported to the police, only 64 (30 percent) resulted in indictments. These experiences also indicate a continuing resistance to rape reporting, arrest, and prosecution. Thus, in spite of Iceland's efforts to provide equal legal rights to women, serious legal problems remain. We will demonstrate in the following chapters that the prosecution of drug offenders does not seem to have presented similar ambiguities.

7

Distortion of the Legal Process
Drug Police and Drug Courts

Drug Legislation and Undercover Policing in Europe and America

Icelandic legislation on controlled substances dates back to 1923, when an international convention, of which Iceland was a member, passed the so-called opium laws, which banned the importation, exportation, and production of raw opium. These laws were largely unenforced, but in the late 1960s, with international concern about drug use among the young heating up, Iceland's narcotics laws were revised and extended to make cannabis and LSD illegal also. In the review of newspapers in chapter 4 we found that the police first seized a controlled substance in Iceland in 1969. In 1974 new drug laws were passed by Parliament which were intended to replace the old opium laws by imposing more severe penalties for major drug violations (Parliamentary Debates, 1973–1974). These laws were officially intended to unify and coordinate laws against controlled substances and to fight against the alleged "use of drugs, which is becoming a serious social problem manifested in scientific revelations of the harmfulness of these substances" (preamble to law no. 65, 1974; law no. 66, 1974). For major violations, a person could be sentenced to a maximum of 10 years in prison instead of 6 years, as provided for in the opium laws.

These experiences in Iceland will be used to illustrate how the United States has exerted a great effort to export its drug control policies throughout the world (Nadelmann, 1993). In the 1970s the annual number of foreign police trained by American federal narcotics authorities increased dramatically. For example, U.S. agents began actively to encourage European governments to integrate undercover techniques into drug enforcement investigations. Ultimately, U.S. law enforcement has shaped the development of criminal justice systems in many other countries.

> No other government has pursued its international law enforcement agenda in as aggressive and penetrative a manner or devoted so much effort to promoting its own criminal justice norms to others. . . . For-

eign governments have followed in U.S. footsteps, adopting U.S.-style investigative techniques, creating specialized drug enforcement agencies. (Nadelmann, 1993: 11–12)

Until the 1960s few European police agencies had specialized drug enforcement squads or prosecutors who focused on drug trafficking cases, but by the late 1980s most European police agencies had such units, and "quite a few worked closely with prosecutors" (Nadelmann, 1993: 192). Thus, "as in the United States, but in a far more compressed period of time, judicial, legislative, and executive authorities in Europe were obliged to address difficult legal issues regarding the distinction between legitimate undercover techniques and entrapment" (Nadelmann, 1993: 193). We will see how these same patterns developed in Iceland.

Secret Policing in Iceland

In contradiction to 1951 legislation separating the police and the courts, in 1973 the Parliament (law no. 52) established a specialized drug police unit to be supervised by a separate drug court (Þórmundsson, 1980). The creation of this joint police-court apparatus, contrary to the emerging accusatory law, reflects the deep concern many Icelanders felt about this new and frightening problem. The drug police were sent to the United States for training in American methods of narcotics law enforcement. In a recent interview in a popular magazine the head of the drug police stated: "Our officers participate in seminars held by the U.S. federal police division in charge of drugs, the DEA [Drug Enforcement Administration]" (*Mannlíf*, 1992: 8).

A committee appointed by Parliament in late 1983 proposed alternative actions against drug use, as well as formal separation of the drug court and the drug police to satisfy the accusatory legal procedures prevailing in Iceland's criminal justice system. Concurrently, during the 1980s there was increasing criticism of the drug police and drug court, including a dispute with the SCIP. The drug court judge routinely granted house search warrants to the drug police and issued rulings allowing for solitary confinement of drug suspects during initial investigations prior to trials. Moreover, the legal ties between the drug court and the drug police required that the court have an active role in investigations of all drug cases (law no. 52, 1973), which was also increasingly criticized as hampering the objectivity of the court's decisions (Þórmundsson, 1979). On two occasions, in 1989 and 1990, the Supreme Court disqualified the head judge of the drug court because of the close ties between the court and the drug police. These decisions would lead in 1992 to the disbanding of the drug court, but the drug police still operate as a separate unit.

Surprisingly, what triggered the disbanding of the drug court was a minor case which took place in the small town of Akureyri, in northern Iceland (*Morgunblaðið*, 1991). The story began in 1985 when a man was charged with failing to observe a stop sign. The driver was issued a citation by the local sheriff, and then, with the sheriff acting also as the local judge, the driver was found guilty and fined. The driver was, however, convinced of his innocence and appealed to the Icelandic Supreme Court. When the court dismissed his appeal, he then appealed directly to the European Human Rights Council, and here his appeal was sustained. Yet by this time, the Parliament and the Justice Ministry had already decided to implement accusatory legal procedures throughout the nation (we discuss this further in chapter 8, "Criminal Court Procedures").

Earlier the *Morgunblaðið* (1984h) printed an open letter from six narcotics officers critical of a recommendation from Parliament that all law enforcement agencies join the fight against drugs, including the SCIP and customs officials. The officers said: "We believe that investigation of drug cases has to be held in only one hand instead of splitting up the work between different agencies. . . . The separate drug police is the most practical thing." But the chief of the SCIP noted that from the beginning of his agency, drug cases were to be investigated by the SCIP, not by a separate narcotics police organization and not under court authority (*Morgunblaðið*, 1984p).

In the fall of 1983, two drug cases involving importation of relatively large amounts of hashish prompted heated discussion throughout Iceland regarding the appropriate action to be taken to curb the drug problem. In December of that year the Icelandic parliament passed two resolutions as a result of these cases—one calling for increased education about the effects of drugs, and the other for a coordinated effort from various law enforcement agencies to prevent importation and distribution of drugs in society. These two resolutions were passed unanimously. The MP sponsoring this legislation argued:

> In a nutshell this proposal calls for restructuring and cooperation between customs and other control agencies to prevent the importation and sale of drugs, and to improve on all investigative methods . . . [because in Parliament] and the media we have seen terrifying figures which strongly suggest that there is enormous consumption of drugs in society and that only a tiny portion of these drugs is being seized by control agencies . . . [and that] drug use ruins the lives of a number of young people. (Parliamentary Debates, 1983–1984a: 1874)

Another MP noted: "Powerful crime cartels have reached to Iceland, and ruthlessly their drug dealers bring their nets to grab young people who, suspecting no evil, subsequently become addicted" (Parliamentary Debates, 1983–1984a: 2255). And the minister of justice made this suggestion: "Monthly we should register all cases of drugs and preferably have them computerized in order to have an up-to-date overview of the situation" (Parliamentary Debates, 1983–1984a: 1423). This recent demand for adequate records shows a new and growing concern in Iceland, at least for drug offenses.

Drug Police Arrests and Seizures

During an interview in 1988, one of the principal investigators among the drug police refused to reveal how many officers worked for the drug unit, arguing that the exact number was a state secret. According to another source (Kristmundsson, 1985: 45), seven people worked for the drug police in 1984, four as investigators, two as regular police officers, and one as the director. However, an information chart provided by an officer in the Reykjavík police department indicated that the total number of drug police officers had increased to 19 in 1996, making it the largest specialized police force in the nation. As seen in table 7.1, the drug police annual reports indicate they have arrested approximately 400 suspects per year between 1986 and 1990. It should also be noted that over 75 percent of these cases involved drugs intended for private use as opposed to sales. To give some insight into the ages of those charged, the 1986 annual report of the drug police indicates that 55 percent of those charged were between the ages of 21 and 30, and 18 percent were under 20. Between 1989 and 1992, at least 75 percent of all drug arrests involved those who were students, laborers, or unemployed, with an average of 40 percent in this last category.

In 1988 the illegal substances most used in Iceland, according to one of the drug unit's principal investigators, were as follows: "Hashish is by far the most common drug and has been slowly increasing. LSD pops up occasionally. Amphetamines in a powder form overflowed the market in 1980–84, but have been stable since then. And in the last couple of years

Table 7.1. Number of suspects arrested by the Icelandic drug police, by charge, 1986–1990

	1986	1987	1988	1989	1990
For private use	304	366	388	306	344
For selling	57	85	80	71	53
For importing	35	39	53	30	47

Source: Drug police annual reports for the years shown.

Table 7.2. Types and amounts of
substances seized by the Icelandic drug
police, 1985–1995

Hashish	144 kilos
Hashish oil	1.1 kilos
Marihuana	2.1 kilos
Amphetamines	14.9 kilos
Cocaine	3.6 kilos
LSD	3,500 doses
Ecstasy	1,800 doses

Source: Drugs and Violence Report,
1996.

cocaine has had its full entry into the market." Table 7.2 confirms the significance of cannabis. Over 80 percent of the grams of drugs seized by the drug police have involved marihuana seeds or plants in cultivation, processed marihuana, and hashish or hashish oil.

Narcotics police cooperate with customs and airline officials. They especially look for suspicious travelers, like those with prior drug convictions. Keflavík airport is one of the major routes into Iceland, making drug smuggling more difficult and control easier. Wire-tapping is used only in drug cases, and between 1992 and 1995, 42 phone taps were approved by the courts. And as a part of controlling the drug situation, the drug police operate a telephone hotline where people can call in anonymous information about drug use and trafficking.

One relatively frequent method the drug police use involves the search of private homes. The drug police have made approximately 100 residential searches per year without a warrant, all of which have been upheld in court. In addition to these searches the drug court judge observed:

> This year I have already issued 60 search warrants, and the most the court has issued in one year is a total of 120 search warrants, which is much more common than in other criminal cases. This is in fact a good method, and it keeps drug trafficking under some control, deters customers and dealers from major drug dealing. (August 1991 interview)

When a principal investigator of the drug bureau was asked about the nature of the nation's drug market in the 1980s, he said:

> We first got in touch with drugs in Iceland around 1970, during the hippie era, when people got together and pitched in money to send someone abroad to purchase drugs for their own private consumption. Now the pattern is different and is becoming more businesslike with a specialized division of labor. One person comes up with the money, another

takes care of the importation, and the third distributes the drugs here in Iceland. And these people do not necessarily use drugs themselves; they are only doing this for high financial returns. This is actually very similar to methods employed abroad. (June 1988 interview)

If it can be argued that the crime problems in Iceland largely mirror those in other nations, then foreign methods of law enforcement become reasonable. According to this investigator, the official policy of the drug bureau is not to give out information about their search-and-seizure procedures. He stated that their top priority was

> to control importation, then distribution, and finally consumption of controlled substances. Most of our cases come out of prior investigative inquiries and only a few out of random search at airports and loading docks. This is what makes our activities different from other police work; we investigate cases before the actual crime is committed. (June 1998 interview)

That is, the Icelandic drug police are largely engaged in what Marx (1988) has referred to as facilitative law enforcement, which attempts to create some crime that might otherwise not take place.

Examples of Covert Policing Practices

In arresting two men in 1979, an investigator with the Keflavík police department secretly

> had two women put a bag containing two bottles of vodka on which taxes had not been paid along with a case of illegal beer in their trunk. Then he asked the women to have the two men drive them to a specific location. The police investigator then sent other officers to this location to arrest the two men for the goods in the trunk of their car. (Morgunblaðið, 1979i)

It seemed that one of the men involved, a taxi driver, had been suspected of illegal activities for some time, but the police had never been able to make a case against him. The officer who planned this event was sentenced to nine months in prison; a deputy judge, another police officer, and the women received lesser sentences. Thus, the court sent a clear message that such practices would not be tolerated.

In spite of this clear precedent the director of the drug police later made a confidential agreement with an ex-convict to work as an agent provocateur to attempt to purchase 1.2 kilos of cocaine from an acquaintance whom he had met in prison the preceding year. The acquaintance was reportedly not at all interested in selling drugs in Iceland (Prosecution v. Steinn Ármann Stefánsson, 1992). But the informant was persistent, and finally his acquaintance grudgingly decided to sell most of the drugs he had, even though he had originally not planned to sell them in Iceland, and had in fact earlier attempted to market the drugs in Denmark.

The director and several of his officers, with none of the latter being told the full story, then gathered to make a major drug arrest. There was a car chase in which one officer was seriously injured. This case created an uproar in Iceland because of the injury as well as the amount and type of drugs involved. This can be seen as an illustration of an FBI/CIA mentality, where the ends justify the means. A newspaper article noted: "Drug police officers had been keeping an eye on a man and gave him a signal to stop his car around midnight last night but he failed to do so and sped away. . . . His speeding car hit a police car parked on the highway to block his way, and a fire broke out." The article's headline told it all: "Police Officer's Life in Danger" (*Morgunblaðið*, 1992a). The leaders of the Reykjavík police force publicly defended this chase as being in accordance with "proper regulations" (*Morgunblaðið*, 1992b).

On the other hand, the head physician of Iceland's drug rehabilitation unit seemed to disbelieve the danger from this suspect and the significance of the charges against him (*Morgunblaðið*, 1992c). He said: "I don't have the slightest idea of how 1.2 kilos of cocaine can be marketed here," because there were only 5 to 10 heavy users of cocaine diagnosed in the nation each year. An Icelandic law school textbook argues that such law enforcement practices are "hardly within legal limits . . . [and] may not be used if only to make someone do something he otherwise would not have done. . . . It is by all means better that a police officer should be an agent rather than an ordinary citizen . . . [and it is] not feasible to use convicts" (Þórmundsson, 1980: 139–141).

An attorney who has often defended those arrested in drug cases argued in an interview (April 1993): "It is very doubtful that this police conduct was legal. . . . They could have avoided the car chase and still seized the drugs." Yet most recently the Supreme Court confirmed the seven-year sentence against the suspect, even though the court recognized that the director of the drug police had not consulted sufficiently with the Reykjavík police. It continued: "It is especially important in this case because the agent provocateur was an ex-convict awaiting a new conviction for a drug violation. . . . [But] despite the lack of consultation it is not sufficient to grant acquittal or reduction of the penalty" (*Morgunblaðið*, 1993k). The closest parallel mentioned by Marx (1988: 178) in American drug enforcement involving injury to law enforcement agents was in Los Angeles, where a narcotics agent was shot while trying to purchase heroin. Even though these two cases are not identical, they both show how far the authorities are willing to go to deter drug use.

Cases Handled by the Drug Court

Given the drug court's very close ties with the drug police, acquittals there were understandably almost nonexistent. The drug court records of case dispositions indicated no cases that resulted in not guilty findings (see table 7.3). Another source (Kristmundsson, 1985: 37) indicates that approximately 1 percent of drug cases have ended in acquittal. In any case, once the court and the police have worked on a case together and brought it into court, there seems to be little further prosecutorial work to be done to guarantee a conviction. Compared with charges of rape, for example, the differences have been dramatic. As we saw in chapter 6, the SCIP reported that from 1 July 1977 to 31 December 1983, of 126 cases of rape allegations handled by the police, only 30 resulted in convictions (Rape Report, 1989: 153).

Not only have acquittals in the drug court been almost nonexistent, but predictably in such a legal environment appeals have been very rare as well. In an August 1991 interview, the drug court judge, who served in this position from the court's beginning, observed:

> In fact appeals are very few, but they seem to come up with many cases pending at the same time. One year, for instance, we had a total of 16 cases being appealed, and it looks like this was being done to make processing these cases more difficult and cumbersome. Defendants are, I am sure, merely buying themselves some time.

This judge obviously saw appeals as unessential to a modern democratic legal system, and also defended the utility of drug police and drug court cooperation:

> The first few drug-related cases we had in the beginning tended to cross many different police districts, and that made investigations and court

Table 7.3. Police proceedings and legal outcomes in drug court cases, 1985–1991

	1985	1986	1987	1988	1989	1990	1991
Guilty pleas (reconciliations)	271	227	301	299	276	297	—
Indictments[a]	39	34	29	18	34	15	—
House searches							
With a warrant	—	65	120	73	79	70	81
Without a warrant	—	22	88	100	88	65	79

Sources: Records provided by the head judge of the drug court and by the drug police.

[a]Nearly all indictments end in convictions.

handling much more difficult. Therefore, this idea of a separate drug
police and drug court came about. On the whole, this has in actual fact
been a good and effective system.

The apprehension concerning the relationship between the police and
the court is well illustrated by one case. Two people were arrested for attempting to smuggle in one kilo of cocaine from the United States (*Morgunblaðið*, 1989). As noted in chapter 4 in the discussion of newspaper articles,
the principal offender was held in solitary confinement for seven months
during the initial investigation of the case by order of the drug court judge.
The severity was due to his steadfast refusal to admit his guilt despite the
testimony of others to the contrary. And soon it was reported (*Þjóðlíf*,
1990) that when the narcotics police asked that this defendant be held two
months longer, the Supreme Court denied the request, citing the close ties
between the drug police and drug court, which made an objective decision
by the judge impossible.

There are several penal options open to the court for offenses against
the drug laws: imprisonment, a fine (which is referred to as a reconciliation
and is imposed after a guilty plea in less serious cases), or a combination of
a prison sentence and a fine. According to legal scholars (Þórmundsson,
1982; Björnsdóttir, 1984), several legal options have been available to the
court; thus, the appropriate severity of the penalty in each drug case is
ambiguous. This particular aspect of the drug laws has largely been left to
the drug court itself to determine, within relatively broad legal limits.

Predictably, the drug court adopted its own standards of determining
the actual content of penalties for each case (Kristmundsson, 1985: 36).
The type of drug, its quantity, and the personal motives (financial gain or
personal use) have been found to be crucial in determining a sentence, yet
the exact boundary between a fine and a charge involving imprisonment
has been variable. On the average, cases involving up to 0.1 kilogram of
hashish or marihuana have been settled by a fine. With importation of one
kilo of hashish, an offender can expect three months in prison and an additional one to two months for each additional kilo. For harder drugs, fines
are not as often imposed, except if the offense is found to be related solely
to private consumption. Typically, the sale of 10 grams of amphetamines
can lead to a 30-day prison sentence, and importation of 200 grams of
amphetamines can lead to a maximum of five months in prison, but many
intervening variables can affect the outcome, such as the age of the offender and prior criminal record (Kristmundsson, 1985: 36–44). These
practices have not changed substantially over the years (Kristmundsson,
1985: 36; Drugs and Violence Report, 1996: 3).

From the founding of the drug court in 1973 to the end of 1983, a total of 2,022 formal reconciliations were made by the court and a total of 217 convictions (Kristmundsson, 1985: 37–38). Thus, approximately 90 percent of all drug cases handled during this time period were settled by a reconciliation. Of the convictions, two-thirds involved imprisonment; one-tenth, fines; and the remainder, probation. The proportion of imprisonment judgments given by the court was considerably higher than for other offenses, which indicates how seriously drug-related offenses are viewed by government authorities.

The average term actually served in prison for drug violations was 5 months during the period 1973–1983, with the longest imprisonment being 2.5 years (Kristmundsson, 1985: 39). During 1973–1983, the sentences imposed were all much lower than the legal maximum limit of 10 years. This relative leniency in sentencing can be partly explained by looking at the types of drugs the police seized during this time period; 98 percent of all seizures consisted of cannabis. Hard drugs played a very minor role in drug cases in Iceland during this time, which may explain why sentences imposed by the drug court did not come close to the maximum possible.

In addition to meting out reconciliations, the drug court handed out rulings on custody while the drug police investigated the case prior to trial. During the four years of 1986, 1988, 1989, and 1990 (information unavailable for 1987), the court ruled that a total of 77 individuals had to serve 1,153 days of confinement, or approximately 15 days per person on the average. The average prison sentence handed out by the drug court during 1973–1989 was 14.6 months for major violations and 5.5 months for minor violations (Kristmundsson, 1989: 19). All the individuals involved had been indicted and convicted of either importation or distribution. The records of the drug court show that from 1985 to 1990, the number of indicted persons decreased while the use of reconciliation increased (see table 7.3).

Survey of Characteristics of Drug Users

In a preamble to legislation passed by Parliament in 1983, the estimated annual use of cannabis was approximately three metric tons among people 16 to 26 years old. This amount was obtained from a pilot study conducted by the Ministry of Health in 1980–1981 in several high schools in Iceland. This study found that approximately 22 percent of students had used cannabis. This information was then used to conclude that a total of 22 percent of all citizens from 16 to 26 years old used on the average a total of 0.75 grams of cannabis annually, with the consequence that approximately three metric tons of this drug were being used annually by this age group alone (Parliamentary Debates, 1983–1984a: 891). The reliability of this figure is difficult to ascertain but seems exaggerated for several reasons. Since Iceland is isolated from neighboring nations by the North Atlantic, routes for the importation of drugs into the country are considerably narrowed. Basically these routes include the Keflavík airport, a specified number of harbors, and the mails. This suggests that the proportion of drugs seized by the drug police is higher than in most other nations with more available entry routes.

Moreover, a survey conducted in 1984 casts doubt on this high estimate of Icelandic cannabis use. The resolution passed by Parliament in 1983, among other things, called for more detailed information in order to explore the precise dimensions of this problem. As a consequence the Justice Ministry helped fund a survey conducted in 1984 (see Kristmundsson, 1985: 65–95). Respondents were asked in detail about their use of illegal drugs. A random sample of 600 individuals was drawn from the national census, all from 16 to 36 years old, an age group in which use of illegal drugs was believed to be concentrated. Approximately one-fourth of the respondents claimed they had used cannabis at least once, with more than half of this group having used it as many as five times. Thus, on the basis of this survey data, just a little over 10 percent of all respondents claimed they had used cannabis six times or more, and of them, half claimed they had quit using the drug altogether. Of those who had used cannabis at least once, 29.3 percent had an advanced educational background and were in relatively high-status occupations, and 28.6 percent were students. Only 18.5 percent were manual workers, and 11.4 percent of those who were either homemakers or unemployed claimed they had used the drug. Thus, the majority of those who had used cannabis at least once were from the upper levels of society.

It is apparent that there is a stark discrepancy between the occupational characteristics of drug users revealed in the survey and the occupational characteristics of those individuals whom the drug police have arrested. The survey data show that nearly 60 percent of those who had used cannabis at least once were either students or professionals, whereas those arrested by the police were predominantly either unemployed or manual workers. Thus it appears that users of cannabis who are manual workers or unemployed are arrested and charged more frequently than those users who are students or professionals.

On the basis of this survey data and court records, however, drug use seems to be a relatively rare phenomenon in Iceland. Ten percent of respondents have used cannabis six times or more, and of these more than half have given up its use. A similar 1984 survey conducted in the United States showed that more than half of all American high school students (54.9 percent) had used marihuana or hashish at least once, and one-fourth of the whole group had done so during the past month (Siegel, 1986: 423). In recent research conducted by the Icelandic Institute for Educational Research, approximately 20 percent of students 16 to 20 years old had used cannabis once, and 5 percent had done so more than 10 times (Kaldalóns et al., 1994: 7). This clearly suggests that the use of cannabis in the United States has been much more prevalent than in Iceland. Moreover, in a European school survey conducted in 26 countries in 1995, 10 percent of 15- and 16-year-olds in Iceland admitted to having tried marihuana or hashish (compared with 12 percent for the survey average), and 4 percent of Icelanders had tried other drugs (equal to the survey average) (Hibell et al., 1997: 103).

Drug Enforcement and the Threat to Democratic Institutions

This chapter explored the nature of the drug controls in Iceland with its highly unusual drug court organization. When drugs became an international concern in the 1960s, Icelandic authorities responded by establishing a separate drug police and drug court early in the following decade. These organizations represented a departure from other features of the nation's penal law, which demonstrates the degree of concern associated with drug abuse in Iceland. The number of suspects the drug police have dealt with is surprisingly high, 400 to 500 a year on the average in recent years. In a society that prides itself on being relatively class free, it is interesting to note that approximately 40 percent of those arrested for drug offenses in 1990 were unemployed, compared with approximately 1 percent unemployment in the general population, in addition to the arrest of a large number of working-class drug suspects (see table 7.4).

Table 7.4. Percentage distribution of Icelandic police suspects in drug cases, by occupational status, 1986–1991

	1986	1987	1988	1989	1990	1991
Unemployed	34	32	37	36	40	39
Laborer	28	30	31	35	32	32
Seaman	12	15	13	4	9	10
Sales clerk	6	6	4	6	6	3
Public servant	2	3	3	2	1	1
Entrepreneur	6	4	6	6	3	2
Student	6	6	4	7	6	7
Homemaker	3	3	2	1	2	1
Other	3	1	0	3	1	5
Total number	380	447	473	439	418	632

Source: Records provided by the drug police.

Iceland's deep concern with drugs undoubtedly has many sources. First, Icelanders have long had a tradition of concern with substance abuse, specifically involving youth, as reflected in the long-term prohibition of beer, discussed in chapter 3. Second, drugs may be seen as a foreign imposition in a nation which has been relatively isolated for centuries but in recent decades has been experiencing deep-seated internal and external social changes. Thus, closer contacts with the outside world, together with the threat of drug use among the young, has caused especially acute alarm. And third, the drug problem obviously has international dimensions that defy simple solutions, even in Iceland.

8
Icelandic Police and Court Systems

Police History

In this chapter we will trace the history and current features of the Icelandic police, including the size and organization of the force, to demonstrate what this reflects about Icelandic society. There has been only a small amount of scholarly work on the history of the police in Iceland (see, for example, Jónsson, 1938; and Sigurðsson, 1949). The first evidence of professional police officers has been traced to the late eighteenth century with the growth of what would become the capital of Iceland, Reykjavík. The first constables were hired and paid by local trading companies, and their duty was to watch for possible fires at night (Sigurðsson, 1949). After Reykjavík was granted official municipal status in 1786, with a population of 302, a sheriff's position was created; he was assisted by two deputies. This practice continued until 1874, when an additional sheriff's position was created for the nation at large.

Initially, police officers wore civilian clothing, but in 1879 they became a uniformed force (Jónsson, 1938). In 1917 the city police department was separated from the city sheriff and charged with enforcing customs regulations (Jónsson, 1938). In 1918 the total number of police officers in Reykjavík had increased to 9 for a population of 15,328 (Sigurðsson, 1949: 5). In 1923 the city police force numbered 15, serving a population of 20,148, then in 1928 customs affairs were transferred to a separate post, and the city police took over Reykjavík's court administration from the city sheriff (Jónsson, 1938: 126). By 1930, on the 1,000-year celebration of the nation's parliament, the number of officers on the Reykjavík police force was 28, serving a population of 28,052, which was a markedly smaller force per capita than found in other Nordic capitals (Jónsson, 1938). After severe labor unrest in 1932 during the great economic depression, the number of Reykjavík officers had been increased to 40 in 1934, and shortly prior to World War II it had risen to 60 (Jónsson, 1938: 149). In 1949, 101 officers served a population of

55,037 (Sigurðsson, 1949: 5). This chapter will demonstrate that Iceland's police and court systems have grown in response to changing public concerns.

Contemporary Police Systems

By 1990 there were 260 police officers in the Reykjavík department, serving a population of approximately 120,000. According to an information chart provided by the department, the force was divided into two divisions. The largest division (with approximately 200 officers) is the General Department Division, which is charged with enforcing traffic regulations and other civil issues. The other department is the Investigative Division. This division has in turn been divided into four subdivisions as follows: crime prevention, with 5 officers; accident investigation, with 11; the city jail force, with 12; and the drug police, with 14 officers. Iceland's police do not carry handguns or any weapon except a nightstick. There is, however, a SWAT team, a "Viking squad," which is called on in cases of emergency, such as when someone's life is in danger. This squad has been specially trained and is culled from various police units to handle emergencies. When activated, the officers in this unit carry handguns.

According to the estimates of a Ministry of Justice attorney who was responsible for overseeing Iceland's police officers in 1991, there were 36 police precincts scattered across the country in 1990 (August 1991 interview). Outside Reykjavík, the only specialized police consisted of 25 investigators. These investigators were stationed in the larger towns. Including customs officials, there were over 300 officers stationed outside Reykjavík, with 65 of these assigned to the town of Keflavík and the international airport there. In addition, the State Criminal Investigative Police (SCIP) had 42 officers in 1990. Thus the total number of Icelandic police in 1991 stood at aproximately 640. In comparison, according to the *Uniform Crime Reports* issued by the United States Department of Justice for 1990, the number of police officers in the United States was approximately 523,000; in addition there were 190,000 civilian police workers. The size of the American police force relative to the U.S. population is very similar to the situation in Iceland. Since 1991 the Icelandic police force has been undergoing organizational changes, especially with the establishment of a new state police unit in 1997.

The State Criminal Investigative Police

The State Criminal Investigative Police was established by Parliament (law no. 108) in 1976 and began operation the following year. The founding of this force was a consequence of the separation of the investigative police force from the criminal court, to which it had been closely tied. Prior to the establishment of the SCIP, investigation of criminal cases was the responsibility of the criminal courts, making Iceland's criminal process largely inquisitory, despite a 1951 law which called for accusatory procedures (Þórmundsson, 1979: 56, 58). The establishment of the SCIP was a major step toward accusatory legal procedures in criminal cases, at least in the Reykjavík area, as well as in all major criminal cases outside the Reykjavík area. The SCIP was divided into four specialized and relatively independent units, each dealing with separate types of crime. Two of the divisions were responsible for thefts—one for property offenses, such as white-collar crimes including embezzlement and fraud, and another for other thefts. There was also a specialized division responsible for tax and bookkeeping violations. Finally, a violent crime division was responsible for handling homicide, assaults, and sex crimes.

The police in Iceland appear to have gained the confidence of the public. In a Gallup survey in 1984 (reviewed in our newspaper analysis in chapter 4), it was reported that a total of 81 percent of respondents claimed to have confidence in the police, although Jónsson and Ólafsson report this confidence at 75 percent; in 1990 this number had increased to 84 percent (Gallup Survey, 1984; Morgunblaðið, 1984t; Jónsson and Ólafsson, 1991: 46). No other public institution has received such widespread support; by comparison the courts had the confidence of only 67 percent in 1990 (Jónsson and Ólafsson, 1991: 45). Jónsson and Ólafsson (1991: 44) also noted that confidence in the police is higher than in the United States and in some western and southern European nations.

The SCIP published its first annual report in 1991, covering the previous year's operations, and again in 1992, 1993, and most recently in 1994. In these reports each division provided a statistical review of the nature and number of cases it had handled during the year. The total number of cases they dealt with was 4,233 in 1991, reaching 5,872 in 1995 (taken from SCIP printout). In 1991, 95 percent of the cases were property related; there were also 88 sex-crime cases, including 17 rape cases, and 124 cases involving other violence, including 3 homicides. These reports, however welcome, provided little information as to the outcome of these cases, whether they were dropped or prosecuted. According to the director of public prosecutions only a minority of these cases eventually ended in indictments.

The introduction of the 1992 SCIP report for the year 1991 pointed out a significant decrease in the total number of cases for that year compared with those of the preceding year (SCIP, annual report, 1992: 1). In fact, a decrease was evident since 1989 (which can be deduced from the data shown in table 2.4) and was especially true regarding burglaries, thefts, and check fraud. However, the total number of cases increased again in the years after 1991. During our June 1988 interview with the deputy director of the SCIP, he observed the following about cases of white-collar crime handled by the SCIP in previous years:

> The total number of cases that we deal with each year has not changed significantly. This is especially true for conventional street crimes, which have remained relatively constant, but I detect an increase in various kinds of business violations of small companies and enterprises, where often you find even elementary bookkeeping methods missing, making mandatory tax returns virtually impossible. We have been much too lenient on such cases and too often postponed legal actions taken against such misconduct. Moreover, I believe our legislature tends to be weak in this regard, by making various practices unlawful but failing to include any penal actions to be taken toward such illegal behavior.

One of the most experienced criminal investigators, who had been with the SCIP from its founding in 1977, told Gunnlaugsson the following in 1988 concerning how the SCIP gets information about crime: "We are usually informed through police reports, citizen complaints, lawyers, through our own investigation efforts, or even from the public prosecutor." When he was asked about the general characteristics of the offenders, he noted:

> We do not see approximately 80 percent of offenders again; they commit an offense and do not appear again. A total of approximately 15 percent commit another offense and then not again, leaving us with approximately 5 percent who tend to show up again and again, mostly for various property crimes, such as theft, burglary, and forgery.

In conjunction with this observation this criminal investigator cited a recent unpublished SCIP study of all offenders 16 years and younger which showed that 63 percent of all first-time offenders came from homes where both parents lived, 32 percent came from single-parent homes, and 5 percent were raised by people other than their parents. According to the investigator, this tends to reflect the situations of the general population. But those who become repeat offenders increasingly come from single-parent homes, according to the findings of this study. Thus, a stable family situation appears to be very important in enabling an offender to adjust to society. When the investigator was asked about what could be done to rectify this problem of recidivism, he stated:

> Over time we have learned to recognize when we are dealing with a potential recidivist, and I believe we should deal with them differently

from others. We tend to be very soft on young offenders, giving them many chances before they are sent to prison. This may be justifiable for most of our first-time offenders, but we should not give too many chances to potential recidivists.

When asked how these potential recidivists can be recognized, he said: "Those who become repeat offenders tend to be school dropouts, do not hold a regular job, and tend to come from unstable homes. However, those who hold a regular job tend to help themselves out of their troubles." Then he commented on ex-convicts' prospects of getting back on track in life:

> To claim that there are no job opportunities out there for ex-convicts is just total nonsense. If they seriously want to hold a steady job, they will find a job. The fact that they've been to prison before is not going to be held against them, except if they fail to meet what is expected of them. Prejudice against ex-convicts is at a minimum here in Iceland; they truly can improve their lives if they work on it.

Criminal Court Procedures

Accused offenders face processing not only by the police but also by the courts. There are essentially two methods by which a society can legally process a person accused of an offense. The accusatory procedure presumes defendants' innocence until the state has succeeded in proving their guilt. On the other hand, the inquisitory procedure presumes a defendant's guilt unless it is successfully disproven (Abraham, 1980). The accusatory legal procedure is a major feature of Anglo-Saxon justice, which involves a prosecutor and defendant who present their case before an independent judge. The roles of the prosecutor and the judge are clearly separated. During the court proceedings the judge remains relatively inactive and does not issue a judgment until both parties have presented their case (Þórmundsson, 1979).

The inquisitory legal procedure, on the other hand, consists of different role definitions. Instead of three separate parties—the prosecution, the defense, and the judge—as in the accusatory model, there are only a judge and a defender under the inquisitory procedure. The judges are not independent arbiters; they are very much a part of the machinery of the state. They actively participate in the questioning of witnesses as well as the accused. Defendants cannot invoke the Anglo-Saxon privilege of refusing to take the stand on grounds of possible self-incrimination. Typically, when the case has been sent to trial the judge is already convinced of the presence of guilt, with the resultant trial largely turning into a public verification of the accumulated record, including any previous criminal record of the accused. The defendant is an investigative object of the judge, which results in a confrontation between the two (Abraham, 1980; Þórmundsson, 1979). This inquisitory legal procedure has been used in France, whereas England adopted the accusatory legal procedure. In this century, Iceland gradually moved away from the inquisitory legal procedure and adopted the accusatory legal model.

To understand how Iceland came to adopt the accusatory method of prosecution, one must trace the development of both systems. In the early Middle Ages, crime was largely approached in Europe as a civil matter, concerning only the offender and the victim or his relatives (Þórmundsson, 1979). The state did not intervene. However, gradually the belief grew that crime against individuals and their property was not merely a private matter but concerned also the well-being of society as a whole (Björnsson, 1959). In the twelfth century, the Church began to investigate and sit in judgment in criminal cases concerning its clergy and others, being at the time both a spiritual and a secular power. The legal procedures which developed out of this Church intervention into criminal cases were basically the inquisitory legal method, which was adopted in most of Europe, except for England. The main characteristics of this method included a judge formally in charge of the investigation of all criminal cases. The object of the investigation was to discover if a crime had been committed and who was responsible. Interrogations took place behind closed doors and were in the hands of the judge, who also served as the prosecutor. The aim was ultimately to elicit a confession from the defendant. The defendant had a legal obligation to answer all questions and could be penalized for perjury. However, acquittals were not necessarily final, and a case could be taken to court again whenever new evidence emerged (Þórmundsson, 1979).

In England, where the influence of the Church on worldly affairs was never as strong as in the rest of Europe, court procedures took a different path. The accusatory procedure was adopted during the Middle Ages. One major characteristic was the enactment of the jury system, which in turn gave rise to open court proceedings. The judge was relatively inactive while the two parties of the case, defenders and prosecutors, questioned witnesses and cross-examined evidence until the judge and the jury reached a final settlement. Scandinavian countries also largely adopted the accusatory legal procedure during the nineteenth and twentieth centuries, with both Denmark and Norway relying on juries, whereas Iceland, formerly under Danish rule, until recently had more traces of the inquisitory legal model than other Nordic countries (Þórmundsson, 1979: 56).

It is interesting to note that while Iceland's capital area gradually adopted accusatory legal principles since the middle of the twentieth century, these procedures were not used outside the Reykjavík area until almost the end of the century. In rural areas local sheriffs continued until 1992 to be in charge of investigations in most criminal cases before hearing them in court. Thus, Iceland seems to have been operating two different legal systems—one in the Reykjavík area based on accusatory principles, and another in the countryside based on inquisitory principles. This practice outside the capital area has been justified by the high expense of operating independent courts in regions with relatively few people and few cases (Þórmundsson, 1980; Justice Ministry and Ecclesiastical Affairs, 1992).

The Nature of the Contemporary Icelandic Penal Process

The Icelandic penal process now is largely based on accusatory legal procedures. A major step was taken toward this legal process in 1951, when new penal laws (no. 27) were passed in Parliament. With the founding of the SCIP in 1976, the Icelandic penal process became even more accusatory in nature (Þórmundsson, 1979: 58). But, with passage of a law in 1973 establishing an independent drug court, there was also a provision for a separate drug police force to be supervised by the drug court (Þórmundsson, 1980: 112). In major drug cases the court was required to engage in preliminary investigations with the drug police. This legal procedure appeared to be in stark contradiction to the general rule requiring accusatory legal procedures and, in addition, contradicted the founding of the SCIP, which was intended to investigate all criminal cases, including drug cases. The separate drug police force is still operating despite legislative changes mandating the discontinuance of the drug court in 1992.

The first basic feature of the Icelandic legal process is that there is a director of public prosecutions, who has had an obligation to prosecute cases since 1961. Prior to this time the minister of justice was formally in charge of public prosecutions, which essentially meant that a politician was in charge of prosecutions—a situation that had been criticized on many occasions for not being impartial (see, for example, Björnsson, 1986). Second, the main investigation of a case is conducted by the state police or by local sheriffs. When an investigation is completed, the case materials are forwarded to the director of public prosecutions, who makes a decision with regard to the next step to be taken, requesting either further investigation by police or action by the courts. The case may also be dropped or postponed (Björnsson, 1986). The state police, local sheriffs, and the director of public prosecutions can request custody of a defendant prior to and during trials, with the director of public prosecutions allowed to appeal to the Supreme Court of Iceland if a judge decides to reject this request.

When a formal charge has been filed and the case has been taken to court, both defense attorneys and prosecutors are required to inform the court about the facts of the case. Usually the judge interrogates the accused individual and witnesses, but increasingly both defenders and prosecutors are allowed to direct questions to the accused and witnesses and to cross-examine all testimony. In all major cases indicted persons are assigned a defender. In all minor cases the accused has the right to have legal counsel, but it is not required by law (Þórmundsson, 1979). Those who are ultimately convicted will be required to pay all the expenses of the defense and the prosecution. If defendants have no property enabling them to make such payment, the state covers all expenses (Þórmundsson, 1979).

Acquittals have been rare in most types of court cases (Björnsson, 1986), which is troubling in a democratic society. The low frequency of acquittals could have two interrelated explanations. The first is that the prosecutors tend to be reluctant to hand out indictments unless certain of guilt, and the second is that in a small society such as Iceland we might expect that it would be relatively easy for both the police and the prosecutor to learn the true nature of the case prior to the decision to prosecute.

The Institution of the Jury

The institution of juries as practiced in England and the United States has not yet been established in Iceland. This is true even though Denmark, which ruled Iceland until 1944, has traditionally used the jury system. Juries are also used in all other Scandinavian countries. Juries were used in Athens as long ago as five or six centuries before the birth of Christ, and they appeared in Rome some ten centuries later. The modern Western world traces the origin of juries to England approximately 800 years ago. The institution of the jury has been praised by many legal scholars for its principle of fairness and abhorrence of injustice (Forsyth, 1971). Another feature of the jury which has been praised is its role as a defense mechanism against any exercise of arbitrary manipulations by a government, since the accused party can, in theory, rely on a jury to be fairly and indifferently chosen (Abraham, 1980). Moreover, de Tocqueville in his well-known work *Democracy in America* ([1835] 1956) argued that juries are the best mode of preparing people for freedom, by making all classes respect the decisions of the law and most of all by serving as a great instrument of public education. He advocated the idea of a jury for all legal cases, both criminal and civil.

However, the institution of the jury has received not only the praise of legal scholars and others but also some skepticism. For instance, Herbert Spencer called the jury "a group of twelve people of average ignorance" (Abraham, 1980: 138), and Balzac once defined them as "twelve men to decide who has the better lawyer" (Abraham, 1980: 120). Despite this criticism, the institution of a jury has prevailed in some form in most Western countries on the basis of the assumption that citizens' input into the judicial process helps secure impartial justice. Yet, as Abraham (1980) has observed, the institution has experienced decreasing use, especially in England and Wales. In the United States juries are still widely used, however, with approximately 2 million jurors serving in some 200,000 cases each year. Both the Sixth and Seventh Amendments to the U.S. Constitution require a trial by jury in both criminal and civil federal trials (Abraham, 1980).

In light of this brief historical review of trial by jury, it comes as a surprise to learn that Iceland has never instituted a jury system. A likely explanation has to do with the small size of Iceland's population. It would have been difficult to establish an impartial jury of lay people in a nation that continued to have a population of fewer than 100,000 citizens well into the twentieth century. Possibly as a means of compensating for the lack of a jury system, the handling of all criminal cases in court is usually open to the public (Þórmundsson, 1980).

The Regional Court in Reykjavík

Prior to 1992 the Reykjavík Criminal Court was the biggest in Iceland. It had eight judges, who settled cases dealing with violations of the penal code in addition to judging other cases. There were also four deputies with law degrees, who primarily settled traffic violations. A total of 30 staff members worked for the Reykjavík Criminal Court. In 1992 the Reykjavík Criminal Court was reorganized and became the Regional Court of Reykjavík. This court receives formal charges from the public prosecutor and then determines the legal outcome. Prior to reorganization, the head judge of the Reykjavík Criminal Court noted that the duration of court proceedings was usually not more than six to eight months for the vast majority of all criminal cases, with many settled within three months (June 1988 interview). He noted that an unpublished study of the criminal court found that approximately 63 percent of all criminal cases in Iceland were settled by the Reykjavík Criminal Court. In addition to settling all criminal cases in Reykjavík, the court has settled some of the major cases outside Reykjavík. When the head judge was asked about general characteristics of offenders, he had the following observation: "We know many of these individuals;

they tend to show up again and again. A lot of them are alcoholics or drug addicts."

The Nature of the New Legal Process

One of the basic principles of the Icelandic constitution is a provision calling for separation of three governmental powers: the legislative apparatus, the executive, and the judicial (Article 2, 1944). However, this legal separation procedure was not fully implemented until 1 July 1992. Even though slow in coming, the changes were far-reaching. First, there was a separation of the executive and judicial powers, with the establishment of eight regional courts to serve the rural areas of the nation (Justice Ministry Ecclesiastical Affairs, 1992). Second, the nature of the prosecution changed as well. Previously, only the director of public prosecutions could issue indictments. Under the new law local sheriffs are able to hand down indictments in cases where penalties cannot exceed a fine, confiscation of property, or confinement during the initial investigation (Björgvinsson, 1992). Even so, the prosecutor still retains formal control of all indictments, but such authority can be delegated to the local sheriffs with the prosecutor giving instructions on how to proceed in individual cases. The offenses most influenced by this change are the numerous traffic-related violations. At least in theory, Iceland has implemented the basic principles of the Icelandic constitution, which calls for decentralization of governmental powers, which is believed in most Western democracies to be characteristic of just and impartial legal proceedings.

In 1997, a new state police unit was established to replace the SCIP functions in serving as a centralized force, with data gathered from the entire country (police law, no. 90, 1996). However, the new state police changed the structure of law enforcement only in Reykjavík and its surrounding area. Police work continues as before in the more rural areas. About half (26) of the members of the SCIP force have been moved to the Reykjavík police department, 4 others to the Reykjavík suburbs, and another 16 to the new state police to create a centralized information center. In addition, a new office on drug offenses, led by the former head of the drug police, has been established within the new state police. Also, the Reykjavík police department still has a specialized drug unit, and there are three drug enforcement agents elsewhere in the nation. In addition, as part of this reorganization, prosecutors have been moved to various police precincts to make processing of cases more efficient; thus, the director of public prosecutions has greatly reduced power. Most cases are now handled by the police until transferred to the courts. Thus, both the SCIP and Justice Ministry functions have been transferred to the state police.

Growth, Bureaucratization, and Modernization of Law Enforcement

During the last half of the twentieth century, Iceland has witnessed the rapid growth of its general and specialized police forces, reflecting escalating press and public concerns. For example, the State Criminal Investigative Police was established in 1977, and the state police in 1997. In general, acquittals in criminal cases have been rare, perhaps reflecting the fact that Iceland is a small and homogeneous society. Finally, in the latter part of the twentieth century, Iceland moved away from the inquisitory legal model to the accusatory model of law, with the last vestiges found in the contradiction outside the capital area and until recently in the close working relationship between the drug court and the drug police. In 1992, however, a total separation between the executive and judicial powers was achieved throughout the nation.

9

Prisons in Paradise
The Correctional System in Iceland

In this chapter we examine how the growing fear of crime in Iceland has prompted increased expenditures on prisons, just as in the United States. We will examine how Iceland's correctional system is also experiencing growth, but without racial minorities and high levels of violence, so much a part of the American scene. For its part, the United States has one of the largest prison populations in the world; in comparison Iceland has one of the smallest. Throughout the United States there is a massive prison-building boom, which is being driven by the highly vaunted war on drugs, with 58 percent of federal prisoners serving time for drugs in 1992 (Chambliss, 1994: 114). We will demonstrate that there also have been increases in the capacity of Iceland's prison system in recent years, as well as increases in security and renovations to make the prisons more modern and spacious. First we will describe the institutions and then present interviews with both prison staff and inmates, all conducted in June of 1988 unless otherwise noted. Finally, we will analyze the characteristics of Iceland's prison population.

The state owns and runs all prison facilities in Iceland. The minister of justice is ultimately in charge of supervising the operation of prisons. A newly established agency, the Prison and Probation Administration (Fangelsismálastofnun) oversees the daily operations of all facilities. This body is charged with ensuring that prisoners receive various services such as health care (law no. 48, 1988). The administration operates to some degree independently of the Justice Ministry, which served this function before the administration was established in 1989. The Prison and Probation Administration is modeled after similar Scandinavian organizations; it had a staff of 11 personnel in 1999 consisting of lawyers, a psychologist, a criminologist, a social worker, a director, and a deputy. The administration makes most decisions in connection with probation and location of confine-

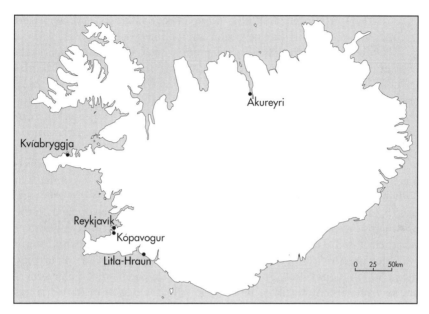

Locations of Iceland's prisons

ment. The first director of the prison administration received part of his professional training in the United States.

Iceland's prisons have been divided into two categories—one type of facility for prisoners serving sentences, and the other for those held in solitary confinement during the initial investigation of their cases. There are five prisons where convicted prisoners serve their sentences and, until recently, one temporary custodial institution where crime suspects have been detained. In 1996, this custody facility (Siðumálafangelsi) was closed and moved to the largest prison at Litla-Hraun, where a new temporary custody facility was opened later that year. It should be noted that prisoners have not been placed in institutions on the basis of their offense. In addition to the prisons, each police precinct throughout the country has a jail for temporary confinement. In all institutions, inmates are allowed one conjugal visit per week with spouses or friends. Prisoners who violate institutional regulations can lose these privileges.

Of the five prisons, one is located in Reykjavík, and the others are scattered across various regions of the country—one in southwest Iceland (Litla-Hraun), one in western Iceland (Kvíabryggja), one near Reykjavík (Kópavogur), and one in the largest town of northern Iceland (Akureyri). Only the Reykjavík prison was originally built as a prison facility, dating back to 1874. The other buildings were all renovated to serve as prison facilities after originally having been planned for other purposes.

The Reykjavík prison facility (Hegningarhúsið vid [House of Corrections at] Skólavörðustíg) as of 1999 could confine a maximum of 16 prisoners in cells for one and two persons. In 1989 this facility held up to 23 prisoners, but in 1995 the smallest cells were closed to make space for other activities. This facility has usually been used as a "reception" institution for initial confinement after convicts have been sentenced to prison before being transferred to another prison or for shorter sentences of two to three months. The largest prison in Iceland is Litla-Hraun, approximately 40 miles outside Reykjavík. Initially, it could confine 52 inmates in individual cells. Ten of these cells have been used for solitary confinement. In 1995 a new facility with a guard tower at the center was opened on the prison grounds, with space for 55 inmates. The oldest part of the building was then closed. The Kvíabryggja prison has cells for 14 inmates and has in part been used for younger, first-time offenders. The newest prison facility, the prison in Kópavogur, opened in 1989 with a capacity of 12 prisoners and is primarily intended for females. Finally, the prison in Akureyri has cells for a maximum of 9 inmates and is mainly used for those serving shorter sentences. The total capacity of Iceland's prisons was therefore about 110 until 1995, and they were routinely filled to capacity. For 1996 more prison space was created with the addition of the new building at Litla-Hraun, so that the prison capacity increased to approximately 140.

As noted above, prior to creation of the Prison and Probation Administration in 1989, the Justice Ministry supervised daily operations of all prisons. In the interview with the director of corrections at the Justice Ministry, who in 1997 became the director of the Prison and Probation Administration, he observed that while the backgrounds of the inmates were mixed, most were characterized by him as "social losers, who come from broken homes and have received less-than-average education." Those who were serving time for drug offenses tend, however, to have a slightly different background, according to the director. They come from "relatively stable family situations, are relatively well educated, and middle or upper class—if there is such a thing here in Iceland" (an assessment that does not necessarily reflect what is indicated by the police data). Another characteristic of this group is that they have tended not to become recidivists. The reason for this apparent reform in their behavior, according to the director, is mostly their family situation, which "puts pressure on them to observe the law in the future or otherwise risk being rejected by their family." Those who serve time for drunk driving "seem to be from a variety of social backgrounds, but most share their dependence on alcohol consumption."

Moreover, according to this informant, not many social services have been available to prisoners to help them adjust to society through assistance with housing or employment after serving their prison term. On the other hand, he argued that if there were such services available,

> it is not at all certain whether that could help their situation to any degree. In Scandinavia, there has been a marked retreat from such solutions because they did not give the expected results, and traditional control mechanisms are reemerging. Iceland, on the other hand, has been sort of undecided which of these control mechanisms should be adopted, but the current tendency I believe is to incorporate traditional methods of control.

To back up this observation, this Justice Ministry official added:

> This tendency can be detected in the relatively steep increase in the size of the prison population during this decade. In the early 1980s, the number of prisoners was between 60 and 65 at any one time, but at the present stays close to 90 prison inmates. Yet, crimes known to the police have not increased substantially during the same time period, but rather prison sentences given by the courts tend to be stiffer today than before.

There has been a steady increase in the prison population in recent years, which might back up the observation made by the Justice Ministry official. Prior to the addition of the new building at Litla-Hraun, the prison system was filled to capacity and was not able to meet the increases in prison sentences meted out by the courts. Thus a "waiting list" of sentenced persons emerged, with nearly 200 persons awaiting prison admission when the new prison facility was opened in 1995. The prison population was therefore increased substantially in 1996 (Baldursson, 1996).

The Labor Camp at Litla-Hraun

The largest prison in Iceland, the Labor Camp at Litla-Hraun, was originally built as a regional hospital in 1926 but was soon taken over by the state and changed into a prison facility, beginning its operation as such in 1929. According to a supervising prison guard, this angered many people living nearby who had volunteered their time constructing this building in the belief that it was going to be a hospital, not a prison. On the basis of the prison's first enabling legislation passed by Parliament (law no. 26), this new prison facility was meant to become a reformatory and a labor camp, where both "prisoners and healthy loafers who are too lazy to do decent work would be forced to work" (law no. 26, 1928: 71). According to this law the distinction between a prison and a labor camp seems blurred, and it was not clearly stated until 1961 (law no. 18) that a labor camp was equivalent to a prison.

The Labor Camp at Litla-Hraun is located close to two small fishing villages approximately 40 miles southeast of Reykjavík. From the outside the building looks more like a large farmhouse than a prison, surrounded by a metal chain-link fence, which is not difficult to scale, especially for young and fit offenders. Nevertheless, according to one prison guard escapes are rare, and if they do occur escapees are usually caught within a day or two. Also, security measures have been strengthened in recent years. In 1995, the prison was divided into nine separate sections with 4 to 12 inmates in each one. For the 70 to 80 prisoners, the total number of staff was 62, including 20 prison guards who worked shifts. As has been true in all of Iceland's prisons, guards carry no firearms while on duty. Inmates work four to six hours per day; approximately half do concrete form work, some make license plates for automobiles, and some are needed for outdoor work on the institutional grounds. In 1997, they were paid $2.50 to $4 per hour. Those who were unable to work were provided approximately $150 per month. Each day after work inmates are allowed to be outside the building for two hours for leisure activities such as playing soccer. Inside the building there is a hall with a TV set and a VCR, in addition to a room where inmates play pool with equipment which they purchased. These indoor facilities are open to them except during work hours and between 10:00 P.M. and 8:00 A.M., when inmates are locked in their cells.

Since 1978 inmates have had the opportunity to attend classes provided by a local senior high school. Teachers have come in regularly to give lessons at Litla-Hraun. Those inmates who do well have been able to attend classes at the nearby school to complete requirements for a diploma. This experimental program has been frequently used by prisoners, and in 1995, 23 inmates were enrolled. Inmates can have family visits outside their cells most days, once or twice per week. Since 1990 inmates who have served at least one-third of their sentence and have been in prison at least one year have been eligible to apply for a 14-hour leave from prison (8:00 A.M.–10:00 P.M.). In 1995, 30 prisoners received 62 leaves, and only on three occasions were the terms of such a leave violated—through substance abuse or a late return to the facility.

In 1988 this prison kept four inmates in security custody who were found to be mentally disturbed. They were kept apart from other prisoners yet not entirely isolated. At their trials, two of them were found responsible for their criminal activity but mentally disturbed. The other two were found not guilty of their crime due to insanity. All of them were sentenced to a psychiatric institution, but since such a facility did not exist in Iceland, they served time at Litla-Hraun, where little suitable medical attention was available. The nation's psychiatric facility was finally opened in the fall of 1992.

In Gunnlaugsson's interview with the supervising prison guard, the guard indicated that he believed that the prison inmates were traditionally "dropouts who come from broken homes where serious alcohol abuse is almost always the norm. Historically, only 1 to 2 percent of the inmates are what we could call real criminals." But, he continued, over the years the prison population has changed significantly:

> Once prisoners were mostly seamen who were hard workers, both here in prison and at sea. Now, however, the characteristics of inmates have changed with the introduction of drugs to Iceland. You can't expect them to be decent workers anymore, since they have not experienced regular work prior to their stay in prison.

He observed that approximately half of the inmate population tended to be repeat offenders, perhaps because they like their prison life: "I believe these recidivists who show up here again and again simply enjoy their life here; they've got their own room and company they like." As will be noted later, recidivism continued to involve up to half of all inmates into the 1990s. When this guard was asked about a solution to the control of recidivism, he added:

> It is doubtful that stiffer penalties could help them any; I think that would only appease the public but would not change the criminal activities of these individuals. Moreover, it would only make them more bitter toward society and possibly increase their hostility. Yet, we should not rely too much on social help either after they have served their prison term. Their reform has to come from themselves, not from the outside.

A 45-year-old Icelandic male who was serving three years for smuggling drugs (amphetamines) from Belgium to Denmark but who was transferred to Iceland to serve his sentence stated the following about his past:

> I have been involved in crime since I was a kid, mostly burglaries, thefts, and forgery. As an adolescent I was already an outsider to society and was treated with great mistrust by everyone.

When asked about what got him into crime in the first place, he said:

> I was born illegitimate, and it was kept a secret from me; yet everyone knew about my real background, and my home life was very difficult. Also, I have always had problems with alcohol, and sometimes I don't know what I'm doing when I'm drunk.

When asked about what remedies should be utilized to prevent people from engaging in crime, he stated:

> Society should show more concern and understanding toward young offenders, establish some form of help to enable them to get back on track in life. There are no serious crimes in Iceland, and therefore we do not need any prisons except for perhaps 15 percent of the inmates like murderers, yet not for the mentally disturbed.

Another inmate, a 24-year-old male serving four months for assault and theft, believed he was being treated fairly by society: "If I was assaulted or someone came up to me to snatch my wallet, I would want to see that person be punished." However, he was grim about the prospects of prisoners when they eventually are released: "The housing situation is especially bad; you are virtually left out alone on the street when you have served your term."

A 34-year-old male, serving 18 months for a burglary in addition to 28 months for smuggling drugs into Iceland, was reasonably content with his life in prison. He felt that the guards generally treated prisoners with respect. Commenting on his past he stated: "I became involved in delinquency and crime when I was a teenager and have served time in prison before." When he was asked about the reason he got into trouble with the law, he stated: "I have always had a drinking problem."

A 32-year-old male serving four years for drug trafficking stated the following about his career in selling drugs:

> I had been smuggling and selling various controlled substances in Iceland for eight years without being busted by the police. I had many customers, among them well-known and respected people here in Iceland, most of them 30 to 45 years old. We are not going to be able to control drugs completely, but we should adopt different methods of control by showing drug users some human concern and understanding, help them realize they are sick people that need treatment, not punishment. I am now drug free, but while I was trafficking in drugs I was constantly loaded for many years straight. Today, I feel freer than when I was outside these prison walls. But I tell you, this place offers a lot of illegal drugs for those who want to use them. I believe the inmates have it too comfortable here, and I sometimes jokingly refer to this place as a five-star hotel.

However, he was not as content with his court proceedings:

> I got busted in 1984, in what was then the biggest drug case to that date, but I did not get my sentence until 1986. Meanwhile I was out of jail for most of the period, awaiting the legal outcome. If you are, however, a foreigner, busted in Iceland with drugs, you will get your sentence in a matter of a few months.

Kópavogur Prison

One of the most recent additions to the prison system is in Kópavogur, near Reykjavík, which was opened in 1989. This prison facility is virtually an open institution, yet increased security measures have been adopted in recent years. Here, all female offenders serve their prison sentences, with usually from four to seven inmates at any given time. The maximum prison capacity is 12, with male offenders constituting the remainder, and a staff of 12. This prison building is relatively new, and the conditions for inmates are in some ways better than in most other prisons in Iceland. Inmate cells, more accurately called their rooms, are relatively spacious, but visits from family members take place in separate rooms. Indoor space for hobbies is available. In the basement a laundry facility is operated, with two to four female inmates working four hours a day doing laundry for the other prison facilities in the Reykjavík area. This work assignment is consistent with the stereotyped, traditional view of the role of women as housekeepers. Female inmates who are serving short sentences do not work outside the prison; however, until 1995 both male and female inmates who were about to end a long prison sentence were permitted to attend school or work outside the prison. After a halfway house was opened in 1995, inmates no longer work or attend school at Kópavogur Prison.

The House of Corrections in Reykjavík

On the other hand, the oldest prison facility in Iceland is Reykjavík's House of Corrections at Skólavörðustíg, built in 1874. The prison is located in a busy business district, close to downtown Reykjavík. The building is surrounded by concrete walls, but the outdoor space, open to inmates at specific hours, can easily be observed from nearby office buildings. It has 11 cells, which are along one narrow corridor on the same floor. Usually, prisoners do not stay here longer than a few days before being transferred to other prisons, but there are some exceptions to this rule, especially if other prison facilities are overcrowded. This prison does not offer many work opportunities for inmates. It has separate rooms for family visits, though inmates have to eat in their cells or in the corridor, since no dining hall has been available. This prison is expected to be closed soon, and a new prison building may be opened in Reykjavík.

Before 1989 no prison for females existed. In the Reykjavík prison as of June 1988, there were three female inmates among the male inmates. If a female made a request to be kept separate from male inmates, such a request could be met only by locking her cell door. In June of 1988, a personal relationship started between a male and a female inmate, with the result that the prison authorities gave them permission to share the same cell. "We do not want to meddle with a personal relationship like that" was the prison director's comment on this turn of events. Female offenders now serve their time in Kópavogur.

The supervising prison guard at the Reykjavík prison had the following observations about the prison's conditions in 1988:

> There is not much for inmates to do here, and those who seriously want to better themselves are usually eager to be transferred to another prison where they can work. But often repeat offenders tend to feel comfortable here, since they do not have to do anything in particular, except watch TV or VCR, or do some reading on their own in their cell.

Commenting on the inmates, he observed:

> More than 50 percent of the inmate population tend to show up here again and again, mostly individuals who have drinking or drug problems, without a job or even a place to stay.

Regarding what could be done to control their criminal activities, he claimed:

> Our probation system should be made more effective, not only make former inmates physically show up on certain dates, but we should also follow a closer social supervision, enabling them to get back on track.

On the other hand, another prison guard argued that it might even be better to let prisoners serve their entire prison term instead of setting them free on parole when they have only a few months left on their term:

> They are released on probation with perhaps a month or two left of their sentence, and their probation conditions are set for one or even two years. Meanwhile, they constantly feel that the police are watching over them, making them very uncomfortable and uptight. Often times they are alcoholics, and their probation requires them to stay sober, which can be very difficult. I sometimes feel it would be much better to let them simply complete their prison term, and then they would be able to leave this all behind and start a new life.

A 24-year-old male inmate, serving seven months for property offenses, said that he first got into trouble with the police when he was 16, when he and his friends used extremely bad judgment and stole the tires from a police car. He was first sentenced to prison when he was 19 and has since served time in all of Iceland's prisons. "The worst thing about my experience is uncertainty. First, they make you wait up to a year for the legal outcome, and then you may have to wait again to start serving your prison sentence." Regarding his prospects after he completes his term, he stated the following: "Once you are released, they just lock the door behind us and leave us practically alone on the street. What is needed is more concern for our welfare in the form of helping us get a flat or a job." One prison guard recalled that this particular inmate, after having been released, was found knocking on the outside prison door and windows late at night, looking for his former prison friends.

Another inmate, a 32-year-old male serving six months for theft, had a different perspective on his condition and argued that his predicament was nobody's fault but his own:

> The system treats you fine if you conduct yourself in a decent manner. The only reason I'm here is basically my substance dependence. When I'm on drugs or alcohol, I totally lose control of myself, and therefore I constantly end up in trouble. If I was able to stay straight, I would not have any problems with the law. I believe that 98 percent of the inmate population are alcoholics, but this is something we must straighten out ourselves.

When he was asked about the prison conditions, he bluntly stated that he would much rather serve his term at this Reykjavík prison than at Litla-Hraun because of easy availability of drugs at Litla-Hraun:

> I want to stay here because at Litla-Hraun you can always have drugs from other inmates. Once, when I served time there, after drug and alcohol treatment, I was offered drugs every day for four months, when I finally could not resist it anymore. They should split up the inmate population and let those who seriously want to stay drug free be kept separate from other inmates. Also, there should be a lot more discipline in Iceland's prisons with progressive punishments according to the seriousness and repeated behavior problems.

The Prison at Kvíabryggja

Kvíabryggja prison was built by the city of Reykjavík in 1954 and was originally intended to be a facility only for those who failed to pay child support. This prison, however, has gradually begun to house a variety of offenders. It is located approximately 120 miles north of Reykjavík, close to a seaside village of almost 1,000 (Grundarfjörður). The prison had, as of 1999, the capacity for 14 inmates in individual cells along a long corridor. The prison staff consisted of five people in 1999: the prison director; his wife, who did the cooking; and three prison guards, who worked shifts, two during the day and one at night.

The inmates spend most of their time during the day doing various kinds of manual work, like processing fish for exportation or performing various other tasks normally associated with regular farm work. The prison building can easily be seen from the highway and looks like any other farmhouse, with no indication that it is a prison. A low fence, not unlike those of farmhouses in the country, surrounds the prison area. If inmates wish to escape, it would certainly not be difficult, since this prison has virtually no security, with no bars covering the windows and without inmates locked in their cells at night. Prisoners are allowed to receive conjugal visits from 1:00 to 6:00 p.m. each Sunday, and all visits take place in their rooms.

The farmland surrounding the prison consists of approximately 250 hectares (100 acres) cultivated by the staff and prisoners. Despite good conditions for inmates, it has to be noted that there are no study alternatives for them, since this prison is located far away from schools. In a July 1989 interview with the prison director, who dressed and looked like any Icelandic farmer, he noted that he had been with the prison for 19 years, initially as a guard. He stated the following about the life of inmates in this prison:

> I believe it to be very important to let inmates do a full day's work, because that is what is required of them in the outside world. I think this is a better arrangement than making them work only three to four hours like they do at Hraun [Iceland's largest prison facility], because once they get out that is all they will want to do. Here, we start the working day at 9:00 a.m. and end at 5:00 to 6:00 p.m., with our prison guards working side by side with the inmates. After the day's work, inmates spend their time doing various kinds of hobbies, like body building in a room with the appropriate facilities, watching TV or videos, playing pool, soccer, or golf.

When asked about the type of offenses for which these inmates were serving time, he observed:

> We get all kinds of violators, manslaughter included, but still we usually get offenders with short sentences, like three to six months. Also, we usually get first-time offenders, not recidivists, and normally our prisoners do not show up in prison again. It is safe to argue that the inmates are selected before coming here, usually those who are believed will not become repeat offenders.

He was also asked about the utility of such a prison in handling all offenders. He observed:

> I believe this to be the ideal solution for most offenders who are serving for the first time, but not for recidivists. They should get a stiffer penalty

than what we have here. But shortly before they are released we should provide them with some facility which resembles a normal household where they go out to work and do the needed housework.

When asked if he knew what happens to his inmates once they get out, he stated:

Many of them do keep in touch with me, especially if they are experiencing some crisis in their life. I know of three former inmates who have not been able to adjust satisfactorily to normal life, landing a steady job and so on, yet have not been involved in any crime.

The prison director, as in the other prisons, gave us permission to conduct interviews with any of the prisoners. Out in the yard, where a few inmates were working, one inmate came forward to be interviewed. He was a 32-year-old male serving two and one-half years for attempting to smuggle several hundred doses of LSD, approximately 100 grams of amphetamines, and 2 grams of cocaine. He was arrested in 1984 (see our newspaper review of 25 November), convicted in 1986, and ordered to prison in the fall of 1987. He complained:

The worst part has been the waiting, first for my sentence and then waiting to be ordered to prison. I had given up most of my drug use, had landed a good job at a private TV station, and started living with a woman. Still, I was always afraid of being sent to prison without a notice. And now my relationship with this woman is history. (July 1989 interview)

Asked to comment on why he got involved in drug smuggling, he stated:

Initially, I wanted to make some big money, like I knew some people around me were doing, but in actual fact, I simply wanted to keep the party going. I had been doing a lot of drugs for quite some time, and I wanted to ensure its continuation.

When asked about his eventual prison sentence, he argued:

I believe it was too harsh, especially if we consider that the maximum penalty for drugs was two years in prison when I committed my crime. But during my court proceedings, the maximum penalty was increased to six years in prison, and my sentence was given in light of that legal change, which I feel to be unjust.

Finally, he observed the following concerning his life at Kvíabryggja prison:

I do not think you can have it any better in prison; you have some privacy here. For instance, one of the inmates is a painter, and he is allowed to

work on his art freely. Still, we are in prison, and I am stuck here. But, I
hope that I will be released on parole when I have served half of my term
by the end of this year.

Akureyri Prison

The prison facility at Akureyri, which opened in 1978, is located at the
police station there, which also manages the prison on a daily basis. It has
the capacity for 10 inmates, none of whom serves longer than one to two
months. Few work alternatives are provided for inmates, options for indoor activities are limited, and the area for outdoor activities is also relatively small. This prison was originally intended to be a temporary facility,
but has now been operated for about 20 years primarily for inmates from
the capital area and Akureyri.

Reykjavík's Custody Prison

The Reykjavík custody facility (Síðumálafangelsi) was originally built as a
car wash for the police but was changed into a temporary custody prison in
1972 until 1996, when the custody function was transferred to Litla-
Hraun. The facility in Reykjavík was used almost exclusively for persons
prior to trial whom the police had caught and had a substantial reason to
believe had committed a crime.

The police can have a suspect confined for up to 24 hours without the
ruling of a judge, and when the case is taken to court the judge has an
additional 24 hours to decide whether, or for how long, the suspect is to be
confined. If there is sufficient evidence linking a particular person to a
crime, the judge can have the suspect confined for up to 90 days while
the case is investigated. There is no bail system in Iceland, and the suspect is
forced to stay in custody while his case is being investigated by the police.
The official purpose of this confinement in custody is to enable the police
to investigate the case without the possibility of having the suspect damag-
ing potential evidence of the alleged crime. Suspects have usually been kept
in solitary confinement, interacting only with prison guards and those involved with the case—the police and lawyers. However, after the legal
change in 1992, solitary confinement has been used less frequently.

There were no bathroom facilities in the cells, which according to
prison guards was beneficial for suspects, since it helped break their isolation. The cells were tiny and had only a bed, a small desk, and a tiny win-
dow in the ceiling. Suspects could listen to taped music and read. Moreover, they were permitted one hour per day to be in a small outside area in
the backyard of the building.

The time period a suspect has to serve in custody can be extended if believed to be necessary for the investigation, and time served is subtracted from the eventual sentence given in court if the suspect is found guilty of the crime. In some cases, especially those involving drugs, suspects have been held in solitary confinement for up to a year. Occasionally, other prisoners are detained there temporarily, such as those who have violated discipline codes in other prisons. When the police have completed their investigation and they and the prosecutors still believe the suspect has committed the crime, the suspect is released to await trial.

In an interview with the supervising prison guard, who had worked there since its opening, he observed that most of these suspects were repeat offenders:

> I believe that as many as 70 percent are recidivists, coming back again and again. However, those who are found guilty of killing another person fortunately tend to not come back.

When he was asked about an explanation for the predicament of these repeat offenders, he mentioned social factors:

> Most of them are born into unstable families plagued by social and drinking problems. You can even find the same pattern among their grandparents. If we seriously want to control their behavior, we've got to face the roots of the problem—their difficult youth and home life. This is becoming urgent because our prison population has been going up in recent years, and this increase is greater than the general population increase.

Correctional Statistics

As noted in chapter 1, Reykjavík and Iceland as a whole have lower crime rates than generally found elsewhere in Europe. In 1990, the newly established government body, the Prison and Probation Administration, issued its first report on incarceration for the year 1989. For the first time, a statistical review of various spheres of the correctional system in Iceland was made public. Even though the first report was not lengthy (25 pages) and did not provide an in-depth analysis of its statistics, it did give some insight into a few notable aspects of the nature of the prison population as well as sentencing practices dating back to 1985. Since 1989 an annual report has been published and has reflected improved record keeping (table 2.6 and the three tables in this chapter have been excerpted from these annual reviews).

As we saw in table 2.6, the total number incarcerated grew from 244 in 1985 to 368 in 1995—an increase of 50 percent. In 1996 the total number stood at a historical high of 417, mostly because of the new prison

Table 9.1. Percentage distribution of prisoners, by status (first time or repeat offender), 1985–1998

	1985	1986	1987	1988	1989	1990	1991	1992	1993	1994	1995	1996	1997	1998
Serving first sentence	51	54	54	55	49	54	54	48	47	61	58	62	47	48
Served prior sentence	49	46	46	45	51	46	46	52	53	39	42	38	53	52

Source: Prison and Probation Administration, annual reports, 1989–1998 (data for 1985–1988 contained in 1989 report).

facility at Litla-Hraun. Prior to the opening of this new institution, Iceland's prisons had been filled to capacity; in addition, there was a list of convicts awaiting a place of confinement. Predictably, once the new prison opened the total number confined grew rapidly. Yet, despite this change Iceland continues to have a low inmate population compared with other European nations. The same comparison exists for crimes; the number known to the police has been markedly lower in Reykjavík than in other Nordic capitals, as was reported in chapter 1 and shown in table 1.1. What contributed most to the increase of the prison population in the latter part of the 1980s were people involved in the crime category "traffic violations." This is a mixed category involving not only traffic violations but also car thefts and driving while intoxicated. According to prison authorities, driving while intoxicated (DWI) increased the most during the 1980s. The number for traffic violations went up from 52 persons in 1985 to 101 persons in 1990. In 1990, nearly 30 percent of the total prison population was serving time for these offenses, but more recently this figure has been decreasing.

Table 2.6 also showed that proportionately the number of those serving time for property crimes and homicide has decreased, whereas the proportion of drug and sex offenders has increased. Nearly half of the total prison population has served time for various property crimes, such as theft, burglary, and fraud. These are followed by traffic violations, which have lagged far behind in recent years. Other categories of crime that lag far behind in comparison are drug-related offenses, sex crimes, and other violent offenses. While violent crime tends to be slightly overreported in the press, media reporting in general corresponds closely to the pattern found in these statistics; approximately half of crime-related news in the paper was devoted to property crimes, and the same holds for causes of imprisonment. The exception is drug reporting, which was overreported by the press in the 1980s, in part because of crimes of Icelanders abroad. DWIs have been routinely underreported.

In table 9.1 we can see that for most years between 1985 and 1998 approximately half of the prison population had served a prior sentence, although by 1996 the number of recidivists had decreased to 38 percent. Between 1875 and 1924 only 6 percent were recidivists (Þórðarson, 1926: 216–217). During 1929–1938, the amount of recidivism increased (Heiðdal, 1957: 161), with approximately 27 percent of the prison population at Litla-Hraun, Iceland's largest prison, being repeat prison inmates. This does not, however, approach the American situation, where in many prisons the population is totally composed of recidivists (see, for example, Marquart and Crouch, 1985).

Table 9.2. Percentage distribution of imprisonments, by length of sentence, 1985–1998

	1985	1986	1987	1988	1989	1990	1991	1992	1993	1994	1995	1996	1997	1998
Less than 30 days	22	23	25	24	25	18	25	24	18	21	24	21	24	22
30 days to 3 months	44	42	43	42	40	41	39	39	42	37	36	37	31	40
3–6 months	21	17	18	17	20	23	22	18	17	16	17	18	15	14
6–12 months	9	13	9	11	8	10	12	12	12	16	14	12	16	12
Over 12 months	4	5	5	6	7	8	4	7	10	9	9	12	10	9

Source: Prison and Probation Administration, annual reports, 1989–1998 (data for 1985–1988 contained in 1989 report).

132

The range of sentencing meted out by the courts is reported in table 9.2. Sentencing practices seem to have changed little in recent years, with about 66 percent of all sentences being three months or less in the 1980s, decreasing to about 60 percent in the 1990s. Only about 18 percent of the total sentences stipulated more than six months in prison in 1990, and in 1997 this number had increased to 26 percent. Thus, sentences have recently become slightly longer, contributing to the increase in the prison population. Yet, length of sentencing seems to have dropped from the period 1875–1924. The average length of sentence was approximately 18 months during 1875–1894, decreasing to approximately 13 months during 1895–1924 (Þórðarson, 1926: 194). In 1985, however, only 4 percent received a sentence of more than a year in prison. Thus, sentencing meted out by the courts seems to have gone down early in this century, only to increase more recently.

However, court sentencing policy is one thing, and time actually served in prison another. In table 9.3 it can be seen that in recent years more than half of the prison population has been released before the whole term is served. According to Iceland's penal code (law no. 19, 1940), an option of giving parole is made possible when two-thirds of the term has been served and after at least two months in prison. Yet there are frequent exceptions, and many prisoners are released when half of their term is completed (Prison Committee Report, 1992).

Recent Developments in Prison Alternatives

The interview data indicate that many prisoners have a drug and alcohol problem and that there has been considerable evidence of the availability of drugs in the prisons, especially at Iceland's biggest prison, Litla-Hraun. To combat this problem, prison authorities have recently divided the expanded prison population at Litla-Hraun into two sections, one designed to be drug free. The latter is only for prisoners who have demonstrated that they are serious about their rehabilitation. In this section prisoners have more access to phones, better pay for prison labor, and better living conditions. As of 1996, more than 20 prisoners qualified for such treatment.

Iceland has recently developed three new alternatives to imprisonment. In 1990 a program was established enabling inmates who have alcohol and drug problems to complete the last six weeks of their prison sentence at a rehabilitation center. Initially only 8 to 12 prisoners took advantage of this program, but more recently 30 to 40 inmates per year have participated (Baldursson, 1996: 45). In 1994 a new law was passed

Table 9.3. Percentage distribution of prison releases, by type of release, 1985–1998

	1985	1986	1987	1988	1989	1990	1991	1992	1993	1994	1995	1996	1997	1998
Completed sentence	59	61	56	55	51	52	53	51	48	46	42	48	39	41
Parole	36	37	43	44	48	46	46	49	51	54	57	51	60	57
Pardon/suspended sentence	5	2	1	1	1	1	1	0	1	0	1	1	1	2

Source: Prison and Probation Administration, annual reports, 1989–1998 (data for 1985–1988 contained in 1989 report).

by Parliament (law no. 55) adopting community work services as an alternative to prison sentences. This law came into effect 1 July 1995, and was reviewed by the end of 1997 to determine whether it would become a permanent part of the correctional system. It was decided to continue this policy indefinitely. Those who have received up to a three-month prison sentence can apply for community work instead of confinement. After 1997, those sentenced to six months can also apply. According to the law, 40 hours of community work is equivalent to a one-month prison sentence, and those who are granted this option will have to complete the work in at least two months. Initially a committee of three persons appointed by the Ministry of Justice could decide who was eligible to perform community service, but currently the Prison and Probation Administration has assumed this responsibility. Most often those who are eligible and apply have violated the traffic code by driving while intoxicated or without a license. Community work has been carried out for various public and private institutions, and initial operation of this program looks promising according to the Prison and Probation Administration's annual report for 1995, especially because this alternative can be cost effective.

Another noteworthy prison alternative came into effect in 1995. Those inmates who are nearing completion of a longer sentence or those who have received a short sentence and secure steady employment are eligible to serve their sentence at a facility run by a private, nonprofit association named Vernd. There, inmates pay a monthly fee of $450 and can hold an outside job and have more interaction with their families, but they are under strict rules of conduct. No alcohol or drug use is allowed, and subjects must keep up with the requirements of their outside employment. A total of 28 people completed such an alternative in 1995, typically staying there between one and three months. Only three violated the required conditions and were sent back to prison. This alternative is expected to be continued in the future. Fifty-five inmates took advantage of this option in 1996 (Prison and Probation Administration, annual reports, 1995, 1996).

These alternatives to prison indicate a tendency in Iceland to replace punishment with rehabilitation in dealing with crime control. At the same time these measures reduce government expenditures in prisons and are thus politically attractive. Most prisoners selected for these programs are nonviolent offenders who have been convicted of property offenses or violation of traffic laws.

The Growth and Modernization of Iceland's Prisons

In sum, prison facilities used in Iceland are relatively small and not heavily guarded. Since the establishment of the Prison and Probation Administration in 1989, a number of new measures have been adopted, making Iceland's prison system more modern and increasingly similar to those found in other Western societies. These changes have included the opening of a new prison building at Litla-Hraun, which has become by far the largest facility in Iceland, with more than half of the nation's prison capacity, or 87 inmates. As of 1996 the total national capacity had increased to approximately 140 inmates. This growth in the prison system could scarcely come as a surprise given the increasing official crime reports, increased crime-news reporting, and widespread citizen alarm. The increased prison capacity, together with new alternatives to imprisonment, has most recently made waiting lists unnecessary; as table 2.6 showed, the total prison population dropped by approximately 25 percent from 1996 to 1997.

Also, in spite of what seems to be ideal prison conditions, recidivism has increased and was approximately 50 percent in the 1990s. Most prisoners and staff interviewed blamed a bad early home life for inmates' inability to stay out of prison. Substance abuse was another prominent cause cited for criminal behavior. Local authorities undoubtedly saw this as consistent with the tough legal policy on drug offenses.

However, despite an increase in prisoners and recidivism in recent years, Iceland still has one of the lowest per capita prison populations in the world. The vast majority of inmates serve less than a year. The greatest number of sentences are for property crimes, followed by DWIs. None of Iceland's prisons can be accurately referred to as a maximum-security facility. Moreover, Iceland has created a number of innovative alternatives to serving time in prison, which have both reduced government expense and replaced punishment with rehabilitation.

10

A New Understanding of Nations with Little Crime

In the beginning of this study we formulated a series of specific research objectives. We have addressed each of them and are now in a position to summarize our major findings. In chapter 2 we demonstrated through the scant official records of crime in Iceland that criminal convictions have sharply increased in this century, at least up to 1977, when the last court reports were published. More recent information on criminal indictments, provided by the director of prosecutions, suggests that this increase has continued. Records from the State Criminal Investigative Police (SCIP), however, suggest that this increase might have leveled off in the mid-1990s, except for burglaries, which have shown a significant increase. Property crimes have continued to be a leading reason for indictments and convictions, as have alcohol-related offenses. To illustrate the significance of alcohol-related offenses, we found that from 1974 to 1990 an average of approximately 2,500 persons (about 1 percent of the nation's population) were arrested annually for driving while intoxicated. Police in Iceland frequently stop motorists at random to test for alcohol use.

Our newspaper review detected no marked changes in the number of crime-related articles per year from 1969 through 1989, with approximately one article in each issue of the newspaper. Property-crime reports were most frequent in all years but gradually decreased and gave way to increased reporting of drug offenses, as well as sex offenses and other violent crime. In 1993 the number of articles increased by about a third for all types of crime. More than two-thirds of the respondents who participated in our 1989 survey believed crime to be a significant problem in Iceland, and more than 90 percent believed the problem to be increasing. In 1997 crime concerns had deepened even more, with 43 percent believing crime to be a great problem compared with 12 and 32 percent, respectively, in 1989 and 1994.

Drug use and sex crimes were believed by the majority to be the most

137

serious crime problems, with concern about other violent crimes increasing in 1994. More than three-fourths believed that either substance abuse or a difficult home life led people to commit crime. Corresponding to these perceptions, Iceland's police forces grew rapidly during this century while the nation has also gradually adopted an accusatory legal system, first, chiefly in the capital area, the greatest population center. We also found that although the prison population has been increasing, Iceland still has one of the lowest prison populations in the world. Most Icelandic prisoners serve time for property offenses, DWIs, drug violations, or sex crimes. Prison inmates and prison staff agreed that substance abuse and a poor home life are the major reasons Icelanders violate the law.

When drug abuse and drug trafficking became an international concern, Iceland responded by establishing a drug police and a drug court. This clearly demonstrates how seriously local authorities view this problem. We found that an average of 400 to 500 suspects per year have been arrested for drug violations in recent years. More than 40 percent of these suspects in 1990 were unemployed, compared with a rate of unemployment in the nation as a whole hovering around 1 percent. In chapter 6 we found that, unlike for other types of serious crime, ultimate conviction for sex crimes has been far from certain because of the problem of proving criminal intent.

The additional contradiction between the rehabilitative orientation toward sex offenders compared with the punitive attitude toward drug offenders is notable as well. Drawing on the notion of boundary maintenance helps explain this disparity. While sex offenses are seen more as internal problems, illegal drugs and drug offenders are widely interpreted to be a reflection of nefarious outside influences. Clearly, many Icelanders believe that the latter requires the utmost vigilance and severity, whereas in spite of long Icelandic traditions of gender equality, the former does not to the same degree.

Consensus and Consistency

If the chapters are analyzed as a whole, some common themes appear. Starting with our earlier research on the unusually restrictive beer prohibitions (Gunnlaugsson and Galliher, 1986), we found alcohol use to be a profound concern in Iceland. We have found that alcohol-related arrests are in the thousands each year. For example, in Reykjavík, a city of only about 100,000, in 1990 approximately 3,500 arrests were made for public drunkenness, and approximately 2,600 were jailed. As just noted, there are also thousands arrested each year for DWIs, and up to 30 percent of prison inmates have served time for such offenses, although this number has decreased in recent years. The surprisingly high levels of alcohol-related arrests lead one to expect that alcohol consumption in Iceland must be enormous. Yet, if we compare the consumption of alcoholic beverages with that in other European nations, we find that per capita consumption in Iceland is lower than in other nations (*Yearbook of Nordic Statistics,* 1990; World Drink Trends, 1996).

Consistent with this concern with alcohol is a national focus on drug use. The newspaper review in chapter 4 reflected a continuing concern with drug use. The editors took a firm stand against this problem and called for strong action to fight it. Moreover, our survey data indicated that approximately 40 percent of respondents in 1989 believed that drugs were the most serious crime problem facing Iceland, and in 1997 this figure had risen to 50 percent. This concern is widely shared by both genders, by differing age groups, by various occupations, and by both rural and urban residents. We found that local authorities perceived the situation in very much the same way as the general public and the newspaper's editors. Corresponding to this widespread concern, a separate drug police and drug court were established, even in contradiction to established legal procedures. In addition, we found that the maximum penalty for major drug offenses has increased to 10 years' imprisonment. It should also be added that the typical substance in most Icelandic drug cases was cannabis (see table 7.2). This widespread consensus on the seriousness of drug use shows none of the elite-imposed quality discussed by Quinney (1970). Further evidence of this abhorrence of drug use was provided by a Gallup poll in 1990: 80 percent of Icelanders believed that it is never justifiable to use cannabis, and 74 percent claimed that they did not want drug users as neighbors (Jónsson and Ólafsson, 1991: 82, 94).

Other points of consensus were found in our interviews with police, judges, Justice Ministry personnel, prison guards, and even prison inmates. They all agreed that crime in Iceland has its roots in unstable family situations and in substance abuse. Notably absent is the idea that social problems such as unemployment, poverty, and other social injustice have anything to do with the cause of crime. These beliefs regarding the genesis of local criminality were also shared by respondents in our two surveys, in which approximately 75 percent indicated that substance abuse and a difficult home life were the primary forces generating crime in Iceland. The public has great confidence in the nation's police forces and generally perceives that Icelandic courts are too lenient. The public consensus has a parallel in the various measures of crime that we employed. We found that approximately half of all crime-related newspaper articles dealt with property offenses and that approximately half of the prison population was serving time for property offenses. News reports on drug crimes, sex crimes, and other violence also closely relate to the rate of imprisonment for these offenses.

Explanation of Iceland's Low Crime Rates

As noted early in our research, explaining high crime rates is a traditional problem, but explaining low crime rates is a problem as well. Indeed, Clinard (1978) attempted to explain what he saw as low crime rates in Switzerland. We are left with the problem of explaining the low crime rates in Iceland, especially for offenses such as homicide, armed robbery, and major drug offenses.

It has been demonstrated that in relatively small and homogeneous nations one can expect low crime rates (Adler, 1983). Until recently Iceland has not had the significant urban population or the high population density often associated with crime (Gaylord and Galliher, 1991). Iceland's population is very homogeneous, with only traces of minority religious or ethnic groups. In societies with diverse ethnic and cultural groups, social conflict and crime are often the consequence (Shaw and McKay, 1972; Vold, 1958), as experiences of the United Kingdom and the United States indicate. Moreover, Iceland's relatively small size facilitates primary group relations, social integration, and informal social control; these are often found lacking in other industrialized nations, which are character-ized mainly by secondary social relations and social isolation. And as Braithwaite (1989) has argued, in small, relatively homogeneous coun-tries, informal community controls including shaming are more effective than police organizations. Correspondingly, in Iceland a good predictor of criminal involvement was perceived as being the breakdown of the family.

Other features of Icelandic society may contribute to its low crime rates. Iceland has possessed a relatively egalitarian and cohesive social structure. Until 1944 Iceland was under Danish rule, which undoubtedly helped create a feeling of solidarity among Icelanders. In addition, the harsh weather and unforgiving natural environment, over a thousand years of low immigration, and a common language and culture may have helped create a sense of cooperation among these people. Iceland eventu-ally declared its independence from Denmark and did so by totally peace-ful means (Grímsson and Broddason, 1977). It should also be noted that Iceland has never had a standing army, and controls on gun ownership have been extensive. Thus, it should not be surprising that the police and prison guards carry no guns. This commitment to nonviolence was re-flected in a Gallup survey (1984) where 91 percent of respondents rejected the use of violence for political objectives. Just as Clinard (1978) noted in Switzerland, in Iceland there are no slum areas, which can provide fertile breeding grounds for crime. In Iceland no slum areas exist because of the commitment to a relatively egalitarian social structure. Other signs of this commitment are the many educational and health care services provided by the state virtually free of charge to the recipients in an attempt to redistribute income through the tax and social security system.

Iceland and Switzerland Revisited

We began our study by citing Clinard's (1978) work on Swiss crime, in which he concluded this was a nation with little criminal behavior. Similar to Iceland, Switzerland has recorded only its conviction rates but has no information on crimes known to the police. In Iceland the situation is complicated even more by only infrequent publication of conviction statistics. In any case, using such statistics, we see that the Swiss murder rate between 1960 and 1972 was 1.4 per 100,000 citizens (Clinard, 1978: 37), whereas the murder rate in Iceland over the past 20 years has usually not exceeded 1.0. As for armed robbery, Clinard (1978: 38) stated that the Swiss rate was 7.7 per 100,000 in 1972; Iceland's court records for the entire 1972–1974 period show only 5 robbery convictions among its approximately 200,000 inhabitants. In 1987, six individuals were indicted for robbery, which then was equivalent to approximately two robberies per 100,000 inhabitants, still markedly lower than the Swiss rate. During the period 1975–1977 a total of 175 cases of auto theft were handled by Icelandic courts, or approximately 60 cases per year, equivalent to a rate of 25 per 100,000. In Switzerland the comparable rate was 70 (Clinard, 1978: 43). We found, moreover, that Iceland's imprisonment rate is lower than the Swiss rate. Indeed, the rate of imprisonment in Switzerland has increased markedly since Clinard conducted his study—up from 43 per 100,000 in 1972 (Clinard, 1978: 116) to 77 per 100,000 in 1988, according to the *Prison Information Bulletin* (1988: 20). This same bulletin indicated that Iceland had the markedly lower rate of imprisonment of 41 per 100,000 in 1988, not only one of the lowest in Europe but lower even than the 1972 Swiss rate. Thus, according to these statistics Iceland appears to be a candidate superior to Switzerland for filling the role of a nation with little crime.

However, there are some close parallels between the two countries. Balvig (1988: 91) has noted that approximately a third of the Swiss prison population in 1983 was serving a term for drug violations, and these offenders tended to accumulate in prison, since they were typically given longer sentences than others. Although in Iceland the proportion of inmates serving time for drug violations (which peaked at 18 percent in 1997) has never reached the Swiss level, sentences for drug violations rank second among Iceland's prison population, reflecting the country's grave concern with this issue. Another parallel exists in regard to traffic offenses. Nearly a third of Iceland's prison population has served time for traffic-related offenses, most of them being DWIs; these incarcerations represent a concern with another type of substance abuse. Similarly, in Switzerland convictions for traffic offenses exceeded all others.

In addition to these similarities, the number of Swiss police grew considerably between 1975 and 1983, primarily to fight the drug problem. The same occurred in Iceland with the development of a specialized drug police. Both nations experienced increased rates of drug arrests. In Switzerland, in 1983, 72 percent of all drug offenses involved only consumption (Balvig, 1988: 95), which compares somewhat closely with Iceland's approximately 84 percent in 1986. Surveys of drug usage also reflect similar patterns. Clinard cited a survey of 21-year-old Swiss army recruits, of whom 77 percent claimed they had never used drugs (1978: 45); a 1984 study in Iceland found that 76 percent of those between the ages of 16 and 36 had never used cannabis (Kristmundsson, 1985: 71), and in 1997 a total of 71 percent of those between 18 and 38 years old had never used cannabis (Gunnlaugsson 1998: 282), which is involved in most drug use in Iceland according to the drug conviction data.

Clinard (1978: 19), moreover, cited a survey of crime perceptions in Zürich which indicated that 67 percent of respondents felt crime to be increasing there. In Iceland in 1989, although the rate of crime was very low, 90 percent of the population felt crime to be a growing problem (table 5.1). Compared with 39 percent in Zürich, only 27 percent of Reykjavík residents felt very safe in their own neighborhoods (table 5.3), the contrast perhaps being attributable to the differing pictures of crime reflected in the newspapers across these nations. Clinard found no alarm in the Swiss press. On the other hand, we found more intense concern in the Iceland newspaper, especially in 1993, even though Iceland has had consistently lower crime rates than Switzerland. Among the Swiss mass media and the public, there has been less concern about crime than in the Icelandic press and public. In sum, in Iceland concern with drugs and other crime has tended to galvanize all segments of society, while this has not occurred to the same degree in Switzerland.

It should not come as a surprise that Balvig (1988) challenged the notion of a crime-free Switzerland. Comparative data from other European nations show Switzerland to be similar to a number of its neighbors and to have more crime than many others. The perceptions of this problem across countries are especially interesting. Why are subjective perceptions in Switzerland different from those in Iceland, with the former being more relaxed about the threat of crime? The answer seems to be related to the differing social contexts. Iceland has been experiencing dramatic social changes in a relatively short period of time in both the size of its population and its occupational structure. The increased crime rates are seen as a threat to the local social order of the society, which is already in turmoil, radically changing from within while opening up to the outside world. In Switzerland, however, the social system has been relatively stable, with the Swiss press downplaying the significance of crime (Balvig, 1988), perhaps in part because the Swiss are aware that their laissez faire banking system may give them a bad reputation in the outside world. Downplaying the significance of local crime appears to pacify both themselves and others.

Variations in the Character of Penal Sanctions

As for punishment of crime, Durkheim (1964) made an important distinction between two types of societal reactions. In relatively simple societies, *repressive* sanctioning is most typical. Here punishment is imposed for the sheer sake of punishing without seeking any advantage for the society from the suffering which is imposed: "The intensity of punishment is greater to the degree that a society belongs to a less developed type—and to the degree that the central power has a more absolute character" (Durkheim, 1985: 129). In a simple society an infraction of a rule evokes a collective response, whereby everyone opposes the deviance. A second type of punishment is characteristic of more developed societies, where crime becomes progressively reduced to offenses against individuals alone, and it is inevitable that the average strength of punishment becomes weaker (Durkheim, 1985). This is how Durkheim defined *restitutive* sanctioning. Here the individual is not made to suffer for the offense, but rather the person is simply sentenced to reinstate the past as it was prior to the offense (Durkheim, 1985).

   In our review of sex crimes in Iceland during centuries past, we reviewed punishment practices that were repressive, for example, offenders being dismembered and drowned. These practices reflected no advantage for those who imposed them, but they showed the great intensity of punishment characteristic of less-developed societies. In the twentieth century, with increased social differentiation reflecting a change from mechanical to organic solidarity, Iceland has gradually adopted different punishment practices more reflective of restitutive sanctioning. The punishment of amputating body parts was discontinued in the early nineteenth century, and the death penalty was removed from the penal code in 1928. Moreover, the length of imprisonment decreased during the early part of this century, and in 1995 more than 90 percent of the prison population received a prison sentence of less than a year. Also, embedded in this restitutive penal sanctioning is a demand that the offender financially compensate the victim or the state. Other measures have been adopted such as work and educational alternatives to prison, rehabilitation for substance abuse, and a new facility for mentally disturbed offenders.

As we noted in our discussion of sex crimes in chapter 6, there is a tendency among government authorities to emphasize the therapeutic perspective in penal responses. In the Rape Report there was for the first time a conscious effort to articulate a public policy toward crime and punishment involving rehabilitation and reeducation of offenders. While measures such as community service, substance abuse treatment, and study opportunities have been gradually adopted in practice, at least to some degree, they have not been adopted uniformly, nor have they become an integral part of the Icelandic correctional system. Still, we expect in the near future a more thorough development of restitutive practices, both because the prison system was filled to capacity until recently, a situation that has already been eased by these practices, and because various substance abuse offenses such as DWIs and drug use can lend themselves to a rehabilitative or restitutive alternative. But such alternatives might possibly generate conflicts among law enforcement authorities and among the general public. Our survey data clearly indicated that the general public demands greater punishment of offenders. This apparent contradiction between the will of the people and the changing views of various legal and medical experts appears to be quite exceptional in a society where we otherwise found uniform perceptions of the nature of crime and the requirements for its control.

Signs of Social Change

There are signs of changes in crime in Iceland, especially since 1970. For example, a homicide occurs almost every year as opposed to every 5 to 10 years, and business crime has become more common, as have drug offenses. The question remains, Why have these changes taken place? Iceland has experienced both internal and external change. Iceland's population has tripled between 1910 and 1998—from 85,000 to 272,000. In 1910, more than two-thirds of the population lived in rural areas, but in 1990 this was true of less than a tenth of the population. Industrialization appears to have affected Iceland later, but also more rapidly, than other nations (Gunnlaugsson and Bjarnason, 1994). With these changes the occupational structure of Iceland has also radically changed. In 1910 most of the population was involved in either farming or fishing, whereas today these two occupations account for approximately only 10 percent of the population (Statistical Bureau of Iceland, 1992). In our earlier research on beer prohibition (Gunnlaugsson and Galliher, 1986), we found that the reapportionment of Parliament to reflect these remarkable population shifts has been slow in coming. Supporters of beer prohibition came predominantly from rural areas, and despite rapid urbanization, Parliament continued to overrepresent rural areas, which resulted in the maintenance of the beer ban; this is a clear example of imposed legislation as defined by Quinney (1970). Yet, once reapportionment took place, rural power diminished and the beer ban was repealed in 1989.

As Balvig (1988) has noted, such changes as population growth and industrialization predictably result in higher rates of crime through increased isolation of individuals and family breakdown. Indeed, there were 203 divorces in 1960, or 4.0 per 1,000 couples; 333 in 1970, or a rate of 6.2 per 1,000 couples; and 420 in 1990, or 10.6 per 1,000 couples (Jónsson and Magnússon, 1997: 217). Divorce peaked in 1991 at 551 (Statistical Bureau of Iceland, 1992). Even though the divorce rate in Iceland may not have reached levels found, for example, in the United States (Giddens, 1991), the increase has been staggering. These figures appear to correspond with the frequent comments that crime in Iceland is caused by broken homes and poor family life.

Studies of income differentials have found that there has been an increasing gap between different occupations in recent years, evident during 1983–1984 (Ólafsson, 1992) and during 1986–1990 (National Economic Institute, 1992), which has apparently had an impact on the public's perceptions of income differentials in Iceland. Compared with previous studies in 1983 and 1986, significantly more people in 1988 believed that income differentials were too great in Iceland (Ólafsson, 1988: 5). Other evidence of increasing social stratification is found in police arrest reports and in prison records. Increasingly, those arrested and convicted are either unemployed or have working-class occupations. The disjunction between social class patterns of drug use and patterns of drug arrests is especially troubling in a society committed to equality. This finding is compounded by the disjunction between men and women in their legal protection, reflected in the difficulty Iceland's legal system has had in prosecuting rape charges. Icelandic women may have reason to believe that they are not adequately protected by the law.

Our discussion in chapter 1 noted that both the consensus and the conflict perspectives shed light on the crime situation in Iceland, much as Chambliss (1979) would have predicted. We found signs of uniform agreement among the public, local authorities, and the media in terms of various crime perceptions, suggesting that a widespread citizen consensus is the essential foundation of the Icelandic criminal justice system. As for the conflict perspective, we found that with a more complex occupational structure in Iceland, income differentials have widened and crime rates have increased. Durkheim also predicted that with greater complexity in the division of labor, crime would increase (Durkheim, 1964; see also Leavitt, 1992). If income differentials continue to increase in Iceland, we would expect, on the basis of the assumptions of the conflict perspective, that crime rates will also continue to increase. And if income differentials do indeed increase, the widespread consensus we found might be jeopardized.

At the same time that these internal changes have been occurring, Iceland has become increasingly opened up to the outside world, making boundary maintenance more difficult. During the past two decades Iceland has become a common tourist destination, and Icelanders have begun frequent foreign travel. In the early years of NATO operations at Keflavík after World War II, enlisted personnel were restricted to the base, in part because these troops were presumed to be prone to drunkenness and other criminal offenses. Icelanders recognized that theirs is a fragile culture because of the nation's small population, making such precautions essential (Hallsson, 1990). Beginning in 1960 through the late 1980s there were a number of mass marches between the NATO base at Keflavík and Reykjavík to protest this military presence. A central argument against the base has been the protection of the integrity of the Icelandic culture, illustrated in the opposition to the military television in the early 1960s. Television from the base could be watched in the Reykjavík area and was very controversial. This was prior to Icelandic television, which began in 1966, and the Americans were eventually required to broadcast by cable to block broadcasting off the base. Later, as Iceland opened itself to the outside world, these restrictions were loosened, in part because the influences of those at the NATO base were not dissimilar to the influences encountered by Icelanders who traveled abroad. As internationalization has increased, objections to the NATO base have seemed less compelling. Correspondingly, in the mid-1980s, the government privatized radio and television, allowing competition with the state broadcasting monopoly.

Moreover, beginning around 1970 there was an apparent influx of drugs into Iceland. When this occurred the authorities responded quickly by establishing a special drug police and a drug court. Drugs were perceived as a clear threat to the social order at the very time when internal changes had already drastically altered the social fabric. This is precisely what Erikson (1966) found to have occurred in the Massachusetts Bay Colony. Witchcraft trials, convictions, and punishment lent an increased sense of stability to a society rent with internal and external change. Just as the Bay Colony was originally isolated by the wilderness, Iceland was until very recently virtually isolated by the ocean. Once Iceland's isolation was diminished by rapidly increasing air transportation, an effort to maintain moral boundaries through punishment was not unexpected. As Durkheim (1964) claimed, punishment serves the function of reinforcing solidarity in a changing community. The deviant individual violates rules of conduct which the rest of the community holds in high respect, and when people come together to express outrage over an offense, they develop tighter social bonds. The deviant act, then, creates a sense of mutuality among the people of a community by providing a contrast to what they are not, which in turn intensifies their collective identity. Being a drug user represents something clearly at odds with Iceland's traditional community standards, which is illustrated by a higher proportion of Icelanders not wanting drug users as neighbors, compared with other European nations (Jónsson and Ólafsson, 1991: 94).

Still the question remains, Why is it that drug use threatens the social solidarity of Iceland? Indeed, there has been a traditional concern with substance abuse reflected in the long-term prohibition of beer (Gunn-laugsson and Galliher, 1986). In addition, drugs are seldom grown in Ice-land because of the nation's very short growing season. Thus drugs are seen as an outside imposition threatening the nation, especially the young. Even though the problem of drug abuse in Iceland has not been as dramatic as that found in other Western nations, the situation is still believed by the people, the police, the press, and the Parliament to require decisive action. The relatively minor nature of Iceland's drug problem is reflected in a study which found that during the period 1987–1988 fewer than 4 percent of all emergency cases of intoxication involved illegal drugs, a significantly lower percentage than is found in other Western nations (Sigurbergsson et al., 1991: 389). In 1985 no known cases of deaths from illegal drugs in Iceland could be found (Kristmundsson, 1985: 61), and as of 1997 only very few had been registered (Valsson, 1997: 102). Yet increased experi-mentation with drugs among Icelandic youth in the late 1990s has once again intensified the public alarm.

Moral Boundary Maintenance in Iceland in the Past and in the Future

As Durkheim has pointed out, not only is crime inevitable in any society, but it is also useful and even necessary in maintaining social order. More-over, an act is not criminal because of its intrinsic character; rather, it is criminal because it offends collective sentiments:

> In other words, we must not say that an action shocks the conscience collective because it is criminal, but rather it is criminal because it shocks the collective conscience. We do not reprove it because it is a crime, but it is a crime because we reprove it. As for the intrinsic nature of these

sentiments, it is impossible to specify them; they have the most diverse objects and cannot be encompassed in a single formula. (Durkheim, 1964: 81)

But why is crime necessary? "What is normal, simply, is the existence of criminality.... Crime is normal because a society exempt from it is utterly impossible" (Durkheim, 1938: 65–73; see also Ben-Yehuda, 1985: 5). One function of crime is to create and sustain the flexibility necessary for the social system to adapt itself to varying social conditions. Crime is functional because it is one mechanism for social change (Ben-Yehuda, 1985). Moreover, crime causes punishment, which in turn facilitates cohesion and maintains social boundaries. At a time of both internal and external change in Iceland, crime and punishment have become especially important.

The precise nature of criminal behavior varies according to the type of society and the type of collective sentiments (Lauderdale, 1976). In Iceland the primary violations that offend the collective conscience are behaviors related in some way to substance abuse. Substance abuse is seen as one of the primary causes of misbehavior, and it is widely agreed that substance abuse must be punished. Thousands have been arrested and incarcerated for public drunkenness and for driving while intoxicated. Legal authorities in Iceland also have taken decisive action against other drug abuses. Even though these criminal acts may seem trivial to outsiders, they are not seen as minor by the local people, the press, or the government authorities. Indeed, the term for drugs in Icelandic vernacular translates as *poison medicine,* reflecting the perceived seriousness of this problem among Icelanders. Even earlier, during the period 1929–1938 (Heiðdal, 1957: 160), approximately half of the prison population had served time for various alcohol-related offenses such as illegal brewing, which reflects the continuity of concern with substance abuse in a nation that clearly can be described as having a temperance culture (Levine, 1992).

The history of this small island nation confirms Durkheim's (1964) contention that some deviance is necessary in any society and that its punishment has some utility in affirming moral boundaries. While this may be generally true, it is also the case that few better examples exist to illustrate the point that the negative fallout from punitive drug control practices is not limited to American shores. By the late 1990s a new drug panic had hit Iceland. Now the concern involved the designer drug ecstasy, a synthetic derivative of amphetamines. Several foreign nationals have been implicated in such trafficking, and it appears that the penalties meted out for these offenses will be quite severe.

Indications are that a war on drugs can threaten freedom even in a small, homogeneous, remote, relatively nonviolent nation with a long commitment to constitutional democracy. Surely more stringent legal action is being taken against Icelandic drug users than is required to maintain internal order or the moral integrity of this culture. Indeed, it appears that far from maintaining moral boundaries, the Icelandic war on drugs contains the potential of subverting this nation's legal traditions. American drug-policy hegemony, combined with Icelanders' traditional fears of alcohol and their experience of recent internal and external change, makes the path ahead for Iceland fraught with challenges unthinkable in the recent past.

We began this research with the intent to understand more about the relationship between punishment and social structure through the analysis of a society with little crime, little social stratification, and, given Iceland's geographical isolation, presumably little need to use punishment for boundary maintenance. The recent experience in Iceland demonstrates that the need to use punishment for boundary maintenance can arise even in the least promising of environments.

References

Abraham, Henry J. 1980. *The Judicial Process*. New York: Oxford University Press.

Adler, Freda. 1983. *Nations Not Obsessed with Crime*. Littleton, Colo.: Fred B. Rothman and Company.

Alcohol Law. 1954. Áfengislög. Stjórnartíðindi: A-Deild.

Andenaes, Johs. 1968. "The Legal Framework." Pp. 9–17 in vol. 2: *Aspects of Social Control in Welfare States,* ed. Nils Christie, of Scandinavian Studies in Criminology. Oslo: Norwegian University Press.

Andersson, Theodore, and William Ian Miller. 1989. *Law and Literature in Medieval Iceland*. Stanford, Calif.: Stanford University Press.

Archer, Dane, and Rosemary Gartner. 1984. *Violence and Crime in Cross-National Perspective*. New Haven, Conn.: Yale University Press.

Aromaa, Kauko. 1974. "Our Violence." Pp. 35–46 in vol. 5 of Scandinavian Studies in Criminology. Oslo: Scandinavian University Books.

Aromaa, Kauko. 1990. "Surveys of Criminal Victimization in Scandinavia." Pp. 76–88 in vol. 11: *Criminal Violence in Scandinavia: Selected Topics,* ed. Annika Snare, of Scandinavian Studies in Criminology. Oslo: Norwegian University Press.

Baldursson, Erlendur. 1981a. "Samskipti almennings og lögreglunnar" (The relationship between the public and the police). *Lögreglumaðurinn* (The Police Officer) 1: 16–21 (Reykjavík: Landssamband lögreglumanna [The Police National Society]).

Baldursson, Erlendur. 1981b. "Viðhorf almennings til lögreglunnar" (Attitudes of the public toward the police). *Lögreglumaðurinn* (The Police Officer) 2: 18–25 (Reykjavík: Landssamband lögreglumanna [The Police National Society]).

Baldursson, Erlendur. 1996. "Kriminologiske og kriminalpolitiske nyheder fra Island" (Criminological and crime policy news from Iceland). *Nordisk kriminologi* (Nordic Criminological Newsletter [of the Scandinavian Research Council for Criminology]) 22 (3): 39–46.

Balvig, Flemming. 1988. *The Snow-White Image: The Hidden Reality of Crime in Switzerland*. Oslo: Norwegian University Press.

153

Balvig, Flemming. 1990. "Fear of Crime in Scandinavia—New Reality, New Theory?" Pp. 89–127 in vol. 11: *Criminal Violence in Scandinavia: Selected Topics*, ed. Annika Snare, of Scandinavia Studies in Criminology. Oslo: Norwegian University Press.

Ben-Yehuda, Nachman. 1985. *Deviance and Moral Boundaries*. Chicago: University of Chicago Press.

Bjarnason, Þóroddur. 1990. "Hið besta og versta: Málsmeðferð í nauðgunarmálum" (The best and the worst: The processing of rape cases). Unpublished paper, University of Iceland.

Bjarnason, Þóroddur, and Þórdís J. Sigurðardóttir. 1995. "Predicting Violent Victimization." Pp. 59–69 in *Ideologi og empiri i kriminologien* (Ideology and empiricism in criminology). Report from the Research Seminar no. 37 in Arild, Rusthallargarden, Sweden. Scandinavian Research Council for Criminology. Reykjavík: n.p.

Björgvinsson, Davíð Þór. 1992. "Lög um meðferð opinberra mála" (Legislation on processing of criminal justice cases). *Morgunblaðið*, 31 May, p. 7c.

Björnsdóttir, Birna. 1984. "Ávana- og fíkniefnabrot" (Habituation and dependence drug violations). Kandídatsritgerð í lögfræði (Law School thesis), Háskóli Íslands (University of Iceland).

Björnsson, Þórður. 1959. "Um opinberan ákæranda" (On the director of public prosecutions). *Úlfljótur* 12, no. 2 (April): 3–14 (Reykjavík: Orator, félag laganema við Háskóla Íslands [Orator, Law School students' association]).

Björnsson, Þórður. 1986. "Embætti ríkissaksóknara 25 ára" (The director of public prosecutions for 25 years). *Morgunblaðið*, 1 July, pp. 28–29.

Boggs, S. L., and John F. Galliher. 1975. "Evaluating the Police: A Comparison of Black Street and Household Respondents." *Social Problems* 22: 393–406.

Braithwaite, John. 1989. *Crime, Shame and Reintegration*. New York: Cambridge University Press.

Brun-Gulbrandsen, Sverre. 1971. "How Dangerous Are Dangerous Drugs?" Pp. 35–49 in vol. 3 of Scandinavian Studies in Criminology. Oslo: Scandinavian University Books.

Carson, W. G. 1975. "Symbolic and Instrumental Dimensions of Early Factory Legislation: A Case Study in the Social Origins of Criminal Law." Pp. 107–138 in *Crime, Criminology and Public Policy*, ed. R. Hood. New York: Free Press.

Cavadino, Michael, and James Dignan. 1997. *The Penal System: An Introduction*. 2d ed. London: Sage Publications.

Chambliss, William J. 1973. "Functional and Conflict Theories of Crime." *MSS Modular Publication* (pamphlet), module 17, pp. 1–23.

Chambliss, William J. 1979. "Contradictions and Conflicts in Law Creation." Pp. 3–27 in *Research in Law and Sociology*, vol. 2, ed. Steven Spitzer. Greenwich, Conn.: JAI Press, Inc.

Chambliss, William J. 1994. "Don't Confuse Me with Facts: Clinton 'Just Says No.' " *New Left Review* 24: 113–126.

Christie, Nils. 1993. *Crime Control as Industry: Towards Gulags, Western Style.* London: Routledge.

Clinard, Marshall B. 1978. *Cities with Little Crime: The Case of Switzerland.* London: Cambridge University Press.

Conrad, Peter, and Joseph Schneider. 1992. *Deviance and Medicalization: From Badness to Sickness.* Philadelphia, Pa.: Temple University Press.

Criminal Victimization in the United States, 1986. 1988. Washington, D.C.: U.S. Government Printing Office.

Davis, F. J. 1952. "Crime News in Colorado Newspapers." *American Journal of Sociology* 57: 325–330.

Drug police annual reports. 1986–1990. "Ársskýrslur fíkniefnalögreglunnar." Reykjavík.

Drugs and Violence Report. 1996. *Skýrsla um útbreiðslu fíkniefna og þróun ofbeldis.* Lögð fyrir Alþingi á 120. löggjafarþingi 1995–96, skv. beiðni (submitted to Parliament, 1995–1996). Apríl, Forsætisráðuneytið (The Prime Ministry).

Durkheim, Émile. 1938. *The Rules of Sociological Method.* New York: Free Press.

Durkheim, Émile. 1964. *The Division of Labor in Society.* New York: Free Press.

Durkheim, Émile. 1985. *Émile Durkheim: Selected Writings.* Edited by Anthony Giddens. Cambridge: Cambridge University Press.

Edelman, Murray. 1964. *The Symbolic Uses of Politics.* Urbana, Ill.: University of Illinois Press.

Einarsson, Ólafur R. 1970. *Uppruni íslenskrar verkalýðshreyfingar* (The origins of the Icelandic labor union). Reykjavík: Menningar- og Fræðslusamband Alþýðu (Cultural and Educational Association of Workers).

Ericson, Richard V., Patricia M. Baranek, and Janet B. L. Chan. 1989. *Negotiating Control: A Study of News Sources.* Toronto: University of Toronto Press.

Erikson, Kai T. 1966. *Wayward Puritans: A Study in the Sociology of Deviance.* New York: John Wiley and Sons.

Estrich, Susan. 1987. *Real Rape.* Cambridge, Mass.: Harvard University Press.

Farnworth, Margaret, and Patrick Horan. 1980. "Separate Justice: An Analysis of Race Differences in Court Processes." *Social Science Research* 9: 381–399.

Finnbogason, Guðmundur. 1971. *Íslendingar* (Icelanders). Reykjavík: AB.

Fishman, Mark. 1978. "Crime Waves as Ideology." *Social Problems* 25: 531–543.

Forsyth, William. 1971. *History of Trial by Jury.* New York: B. Franklin.

Galliher, John F. 1991. "The Willie Horton Fact, Faith, and Commonsense Theory of Crime." Pp. 245–250 in *Criminology as Peacemaking,* ed. Harold E. Pepinsky and Richard Quinney. Bloomington, Ind.: Indiana University Press.

Galliher, John F., and John R. Cross. 1982. "Symbolic Severity in the Land of Easy Virtue: Nevada's High Marihuana Penalty." *Social Problems* 29: 380–386.

Galliher, John F., and John R. Cross. 1983. *Morals Legislation without Morality: The Case of Nevada.* New Brunswick, N.J.: Rutgers University Press.

Gallup survey. 1984. "Mest traust á lögreglu—minnst á dagblöðunum" (Most confidence in the police—least in the press). *Morgunblaðið,* 22 November, p. 36.

156   References

Gaylord, Mark, and John F. Galliher. 1991. "Riding the Underground Dragon: Crime Control and Public Order on Hong Kong's Mass Transit Railway." *British Journal of Criminology* 31: 15–25.

Giddens, Anthony. 1991. *Introduction to Sociology*. New York: W. W. Norton and Company.

Grímsson, Ólafur Ragnar, and Þorbjörn Broddason. 1977. *Íslenska þjóðfélagið* (Icelandic society). Reykjavík: Félagsvísindadeild Háskóla Íslands og Örn og Örlygur (Faculty of Social Science and Örn and Örlygur).

Guðjónsson, Gísli H. 1982a. "Delinquent Boys in Reykjavík: A Follow-up Study of Boys Sent to an Institution." Pp. 203–212 in *Abnormal Offenders, Delinquency and the Criminal Justice System*, ed. John Gunn and David P. Farrington. New York: John Wiley and Sons, Inc.

Guðjónsson, Gísli H. 1982b. "The Nature of Shoplifting in Iceland." *Forensic Science International* 19: 209–216.

Guðjónsson, Gísli, and Hannes Pétursson. 1984. "Psychiatric Court Reports in Iceland 1970–1982." *Acta Psychiatry Scandinavia* 70: 44–49.

Guðjónsson, Gísli, and Hannes Pétursson. 1990. "Homicide in the Nordic Countries." *Acta Psychiatry Scandinavia* 82: 49–54.

Gunnlaugsson, Helgi. 1998. "Narkotikabruk, attityder och kontrollpolitik i Island: En jämförelse med det övriga Norden" (Drug use, attitudes and control policies in Iceland: Comparison with the other Nordic countries). *Nordisk alkohol- & narkotikatidskrift* (Nordic Studies on Alcohol and Drugs) 15 (5–6): 278–287 (Helsinki).

Gunnlaugsson, Helgi, and Þóroddur Bjarnason. 1994. "Establishing a Discipline: The Impact of Society on the Development of Icelandic Sociology." *Acta Sociologica* 37: 303–312.

Gunnlaugsson, Helgi, and John F. Galliher. 1986. "Prohibition of Beer in Iceland: An International Test of Symbolic Politics." *Law and Society Review* 20: 335–353.

Gunnlaugsson, Helgi, and John F. Galliher. 1995. "The Secret Drug Police of Iceland." Pp. 235–247 in *Undercover: Police Surveillance in Comparative Perspective*, ed. Cyrille Fijnaut and Gary Marx. The Hague: Kluwer Law International.

Gusfield, Joseph R. 1955. "Social Structure and Moral Reform: A Study of the Woman's Christian Temperance Union." *American Journal of Sociology* 61: 221–232.

Gusfield, Joseph R. 1963. *Symbolic Crusade: Status Politics and the American Temperance Movement*. Urbana, Ill.: University of Illinois Press.

Gusfield, Joseph R. 1967. "Moral Passage: The Symbolic Process in Public Designations of Deviance." *Social Problems* 15: 175–188.

Hagan, John, John D. Hewitt, and Duane F. Alwin. 1979. "Ceremonial Justice: Crime and Punishment in a Loosely Coupled System." *Social Forces* 58: 506–527.

Hallsson, Friðrik Haukur. 1990. *Herstöðin: Félagslegt umhverfi og íslenskt þjóðlíf* (The military base: Social environment and Icelandic social life). Akureyri: Forlag höfundanna.

Harðardóttir, Ragnheiður. 1991. "Um brot gegn 211. grein Almennra hegningarlaga" (On the violation of Article 211 in the Icelandic penal code). *Úlfljótur* 44 (1): 43–54 (Reykjavík: Orator, félag laganema við Háskóla Íslands [Orator, Law School students' association]).

Harðarson, Ólafur Þ. 1983. Unpublished survey findings (in Icelandic). Faculty of Social Science, University of Iceland.

Hauge, Ragnar. 1965. "Crime and the Press." Pp. 147–164 in vol. 1 of Scandinavian Studies in Criminology. Oslo: Scandinavian University Books.

Hauge, Ragnar, and Preben Wolf. 1974. "Criminal Violence in Three Scandinavian Countries." Pp. 25–34 in vol. 5 of Scandinavian Studies in Criminology. Oslo: Scandinavian University Books.

Heiðdal, Sigurður. 1957. *Örlög á Litla-Hrauni* (Destiny at Litla-Hraun). Reykjavík: Iðunn.

Helgason, Jón. 1960. *Öldin átjánda: Minnisverð tíðindi 1701–1760* (The eighteenth century: Memorable reports 1701–1760). Reykjavík: Iðunn.

Helgason, Jón. 1980. *Öldin sextánda: Minnisverð tíðindi 1501–1550* (The sixteenth century: Memorable reports 1501–1550). Reykjavík: Iðunn.

Hibell, Björn, Barbro Andersson, Þóroddur Bjarnason, Anna Kokkevi, Mark Morgan, and Anu Narusk. 1997. The ESPAD Report: Alcohol and Other Drug Use among students in 26 European Countries. Stockholm: CAN.

Himmelstein, Jerome L. 1983. *The Strange Career of Marihuana: Politics and Ideology of Drug Control in America*. Westport, Conn.: Greenwood Press.

Icelandic Tourist Board. 1996. Ferðamálaráð Íslands. Unpublished tourism statistics (in Icelandic). Reykjavík.

Ingvarsson, Lúðvík. 1970. *Refsingar á Íslandi á þjóðveldistímanum* (Punishment in the Commonwealth of Iceland). Reykjavík: Menningarsjóður.

Interpol. 1993. *Annual Report*. Lyon, France.

Jochens, Jenny. 1995. *Women in Old Norse Society*. Ithaca, N.Y.: Cornell University Press.

Jónsson, Guðbrandur. 1938. *Lögreglan í Reykjavík* (The Reykjavík police). Reykjavík: Lögreglustjórnin í Reykjavík.

Jónsson, Guðmundur, and Magnús Magnússon, eds. 1997. *Hagskinna* (Icelandic historical statistics). Reykjavík: Hagstofa Íslands.

Jónsson, Friðrik H., and Stefán Ólafsson. 1991. *Úr lífsgildakönnun 1990: Lífsskoðun í nútímalegum þjóðfélögum* (Value study 1990: Values in modern societies). Reykjavík: Félagsvísindastofnun Háskóla Íslands (Social Science Research Institute of the University of Iceland).

Joutsen, Matti. 1992. "Developments in Delinquency and Criminal Justice: Nordic Perspective." Pp. 23–43 in *Crime and Control in Comparative Perspectives*, ed. Hans-Gunther Heiland, Louise I. Shelley, and Hisao Kotoh. New York: Walter de Gruyter.

Justice Ministry and Ecclesiastical Affairs. 1992. Dóms- og kirkjumálaráðuneytið. *Aðskilnaður dómsvalds og umboðsvalds í héraði* (Separation of judicial and executive powers in the countryside). Reykjavík.

Justice Statistics, 1913–1918. 1927. *Dómsmálaskýrslur: Hagstofa Íslands*. Hagstofan (Statistical Bureau of Iceland). Reykjavík: Gutenberg.

Justice Statistics, 1881–1925. 1930. *Dómsmálaskýrslur: Hagstofa Íslands*. Hagstofan (Statistical Bureau of Iceland). Reykjavík: Gutenberg.

Justice Statistics, 1946–1952. 1958. *Dómsmálaskýrslur: Hagstofa Íslands*. Hagstofan (Statistical Bureau of Iceland). Reykjavík: Gutenberg.

Justice Statistics, 1966–1968. 1973. *Dómsmálaskýrslur: Hagstofa Íslands*. Hagstofan (Statistical Bureau of Iceland). Reykjavík: Gutenberg.

Justice Statistics, 1969–1971. 1975. *Dómsmálaskýrslur: Hagstofa Íslands*. Hagstofan (Statistical Bureau of Iceland). Reykjavík: Gutenberg.

Justice Statistics, 1972–1974. 1978. *Dómsmálaskýrslur: Hagstofa Íslands*. Hagstofan (Statistical Bureau of Iceland). Reykjavík: Gutenberg.

Justice Statistics, 1975–1977. 1983. *Dómsmálaskýrslur: Hagstofa Íslands*. Hagstofan (Statistical Bureau of Iceland). Reykjavík: Gutenberg.

Kaldalóns, Ingibjörg, Þórdís Sigurðardóttir, and Þóroddur Bjarnason. 1994. *Vímuefnaneysla framhaldsskólanema 1992–94* (Substance use among senior high school students in 1992–94). Reykjavík: Rannsóknastofnun uppeldis- og menntamála (Icelandic Institute for Educational Research).

Kaplan, John. 1970. *Marihuana—The New Prohibition*. New York: World Publishing Company.

Kristjánsson, Svanur. 1977. *Íslensk verkalýðshreyfing 1920–1930* (Icelandic labor unions 1920–1930). Reykjavík: Félagsvísindadeild Háskóla Íslands og Örn og Örlygur (Faculty of Social Science of the University of Iceland and Örn and Örlygur).

Kristmundsson, Ómar H. 1985. *Ólögleg ávana- og fíkniefni á Íslandi* (Illicit drugs of habituation and dependence in Iceland). Reykjavík: Dóms- og kirkjumálaráðuneytið (The Justice Ministry and Ecclesiastical Affairs).

Kristmundsson, Ómar H. 1989. *Refsivistardómar og fullnusta þeirra gæsluvarðhald: Tölfræðilegt yfirlit* (Penal sentences, their completion and custody: A statistical account). Reykjavík: Dóms- og kirkjumálaráðuneytið (The Justice Ministry and Ecclesiastical Affairs).

Kutschinsky, Berl. 1968. "Knowledge and Attitudes Concerning Legal Phenomena in Denmark." Pp. 125–160 in vol. 2: *Aspects of Social Control in Welfare States*, ed. Nils Christie, of Scandinavian Studies in Criminology. Oslo: Scandinavian University Books.

Lasley, J. R. 1994. "The Impact of the Rodney King Incident on Citizen Attitudes toward Police." *Policing and Society* 3: 245–255.

Lauderdale, Pat. 1976. "Deviance and Moral Boundaries." *American Sociological Review* 41: 660–676.

Leavitt, Gregory C. 1992. "General Evolution and Durkheim's Hypothesis of Crime Frequency: A Cross-Cultural Test." *Sociological Quarterly* 33: 241–263.

Lenke, Leif. 1980. "Criminal Policy and Repression in Capitalist Societies—The Scandinavian Case." Pp. 5–30 in vol. 7: *Policing Scandinavia*, ed. Ragnar Hauge, of Scandinavian Studies in Criminology. Oslo: Scandinavian University Books.

Levine, Harry G. 1992. "Temperance Culture: Concerns about Alcohol Problems in Nordic- and English-speaking Cultures." Pp. 15–36 in *The Nature of Alco-*

hol and Drug Related Problems, ed. G. Edwards and M. Lader. London: Oxford University Press.

Liska, Alan E. 1987. "A Critical Examination of Macro Perspectives on Crime Control." *Annual Review of Sociology* 13: 67–88.

Little, Craig B. 1983. *Understanding Deviance and Control: Theory, Research and Social Policy.* New York: F. E. Peacock Publishers.

Mackinnon, Catharine A. 1989. *Toward a Feminist Theory of the State.* Cambridge, Mass.: Harvard University Press.

Mannlíf. 1992. "Stríðið við sölumenn dauðans" (The war against the dealers of death). Vol. 9, no. 9 (November): 6–15 (Reykjavík).

Marquart, James W., and Ben M. Crouch. 1985. "Judicial Reform and Prisoner Control: The Impact of *Ruiz v. Estelle* on the Texas Penitentiary." *Law and Society Review* 19: 557–586.

Marx, Gary T. 1988. *Undercover: Police Surveillance in America.* Berkeley, Calif.: University of California Press.

McCaghy, Charles H. 1985. *Deviant Behavior: Crime, Conflict, and Interest Groups.* 2d ed. New York: Macmillan.

McLeod, Jack M., Mira Sotirovic, William P. Eveland, Jr., Zhongshi Guo, Edward M. Horowitz, Patricia Moy, and Katie Daily. 1996. "Let the Punishment Fit the (Perceptions of) Crime: Effects of Local Television News on Evaluations of Crime Policy Proposals." Paper presented at the meetings of the International Communication Association, Chicago.

Miller, William Ian. 1990. *Bloodtaking and Peacemaking: Feud, Law, and Society in Saga Iceland.* Chicago: University of Chicago Press.

Morgan, Patricia A. 1978. "The Legislation of Drug Law: Economic and Social Control." *Journal of Drug Issues* 8: 53–62.

Myers, Martha A. 1979–1980. "Predicting the Behavior of Law: A Test of Two Models." *Law and Society Review* 14: 835–857.

Nadelmann, Ethan A. 1993. *Cops across Borders: The Internationalization of U.S. Criminal Law Enforcement.* University Park, Pa.: Pennsylvania State University Press.

National Economic Institute. 1992. Þjóðhagsstofnun. *Dreifing atvinnutekna 1986–1990* (Distribution of salaried income 1986–1990). Report no. 7, June. Reykjavík.

Nordal, Sigurður. 1990. *Icelandic Culture.* Translated by Vilhjalmur T. Bjarnar. Ithaca, N.Y.: Cornell University Press.

Ólafsdóttir, Hildigunnur. 1985. "Kriminalitetstendenser i Island" (Criminal tendencies in Iceland). *Nordisk tidsskrift for kriminalvidenskap* (Nordic Journal of Criminology) 72, no. 2 (April): 81–100.

Ólafsdóttir, Hildigunnur, and Tómas Helgason. 1988. "Innlagnir á meðferðarstofnanir vegna misnotkunar áfengis og annarra vímuefna 1975–1985" (Admissions for treatment of alcohol and drug abuse 1975–1985). *Læknablaðið* (The Icelandic Medical Journal) 74 (4): 165–167.

Ólafsson, Stefán. 1988. "Viðhorf Íslendinga til tekjuskiptingar" (Attitudes of Icelanders toward income differentials). *BHMR-tíðindi* 1 (4): 4–10 (Reykjavík).

Ólafsson, Stefán. 1992. "Hafið er auðugt en fiskimennirnir fátækir: Um tekjuskiptingu á Íslandi" (The ocean is rich but the fishermen are poor: On income differences in Iceland). *Vísbending* 10, no. 21 (June) (Reykjavík; a weekly newsletter on business and economic affairs).

Parker, Keith D., Anne B. Onyekwuluje, and Komanduri S. Murty. 1995. "African Americans' Attitudes toward the Local Police: A Multivariate Analysis." *Journal of Black Studies* 25: 396–409.

Parliamentary Debates. 1932–1933. Alþingistíðindi. Þingskjöl A (part A).

Parliamentary Debates. 1934–1935. Alþingistíðindi. Part B, no. 7.

Parliamentary Debates. 1940–1941. Alþingistíðindi. Part B, no. 18.

Parliamentary Debates. 1946–1947. Alþingistíðindi. Part A, nos. 69–71.

Parliamentary Debates. 1960–1961. Alþingistíðindi. Part C, no. 1.

Parliamentary Debates. 1973–1974. Alþingistíðindi. Part A, no. 588. Frumvarp til laga um ávana- og fíkniefni (Law proposal on drugs of habituation and dependence).

Parliamentary Debates. 1983–1984a. Alþingistíðindi. Þingskjöl A. Tillaga til þingsályktunar, greinargerð (125. mál). (160. proposal, preamble, no. 125). Alþingistíðindi. Part B. 125. mál (þingskj. 160) (case no. 125, file 160).

Parliamentary Debates. 1983–1984b. Alþingistíðindi. Part B, 4961–4962, 4965.

Parliamentary Debates. 1983–1984c. Alþingistíðindi. Part B, no. 17.

Parliamentary Debates. 1984–1985. Alþingistíðindi. Part A, no. 575; part B, debates.

Parliamentary Debates. 1985–1986. Alþingistíðindi. Part B, 3082–3083, 4525.

Parliamentary Debates. 1987–1988a. Alþingistíðindi. Part B, 445.

Parliamentary Debates. 1987–1988b. Alþingistíðindi. Part B, 4777, no. 18.

Parliamentary Files. 1993–1994. Þingskjöl. Mál nr. 224 og 225 (case nos. 224 and 225). Svar dómsmálaráðherra (nr. 491 og 492) við fyrirspurn þingmanns Kvennalista (nr. 251 og 252) (response [nos. 491 and 492] by the minister of justice to a request made by a member of the Women's Alliance [nos. 251 and 252]).

Pétursson, Hannes, and Gísli H. Guðjónsson. 1981. "Psychiatric Aspects of Homicide." *Acta Psychiatry Scandinavia* 64: 363–372.

Platt, Anthony M. 1977. *The Child Savers: The Invention of Delinquency.* 2d ed. Chicago: University of Chicago Press.

Preamble to proposal no. 138. 1983–1984. Greinargerð með þingsályktunartillögu um þjóðaratkvæði um bjórinn nr. 138. Alþingi.

Prison and Probation Administration, annual reports. 1989–1998. *Ársskýrslur Fangelsismálastofnunar ríkisins.* Reykjavík.

Prison Committee Report to the Minister of Justice on Urgent Problems and Future Policy. 1992. *Skýrsla fangelsismálanefndar til dómsmálaráðherra um stöðu fangelsismála í dag, tillögur um brýnar úrbætur og stefnumörkun til framtíðar.* March, Reykjavík.

Prison Information Bulletin. 1988. No. 11, June, The European Council, Strasbourg Cedex, France.

Prosecution v. Steinn Ármann Stefánsson. 1992. *Ákæruvaldið gegn Steini Ármanni Stefánssyni.* No. S-105 1992. Reykjavík, 4 December.

Quinney, Richard. 1970. *The Social Reality of Crime.* Boston: Little, Brown.

Rape Report. 1989. *Skýrsla nauðgunarmálanefndar.* Reykjavík: Dómsmálaráðuneytið (The Justice Ministry).

Roberts, David, and Jon Krakauer. 1990. *Iceland: Land of the Sagas.* New York: Harry N. Abrams.

Roberts, Julian V., and Loretta J. Stalans. 1997. *Public Opinion, Crime, and Criminal Justice.* Boulder, Colo.: Westview Press.

Russell, Diane. 1985. *The Politics of Rape.* New York: Stein and Day.

Sæmundsson, Matthías V. 1990. "Leikhús sársaukans" (Theater of pain). *Morgunblaðið,* 23 June, p. 2B.

Schwartz, Richard D. 1954. "Social Factors in the Development of Legal Control: A Case Study of Two Israeli Settlements." *Yale Law Journal* 63: 471–491.

Shaw, Clifford, and Henry McKay. 1972. *Juvenile Delinquency and Urban Areas.* Rev. ed. Chicago: University of Chicago Press.

Siegel, Larry J. 1986. *Criminology.* 2d ed. St. Paul, Minn.: West Publishing Company.

Siegel, Larry J. 1995. *Criminology.* 4th ed. St. Paul, Minn.: West Publishing Company.

Sigurbergsson, Friðrik, Guðmundur Oddsson, and Jakob Kristinsson. 1991. "Rannsóknir á lyfjaeitrunum á Borgarspítala 1987–1988: Þáttur ólöglegra ávana- og fíkniefna í lyfjaeitrunum" (Research on intoxications at Borgarspítali City Hospital: The role of illicit drugs of habituation and dependence in intoxications). *Læknablaðið* (The Icelandic Medical Journal) 10 (December): 384–390.

Sigurðsson, Sigurjón. 1949. "Lögreglan í Reykjavík" (The Reykjavík police). *Úlfljótur* 3 (3): 3–6 (Reykjavík: Orator, félag laganema við Háskóla Íslands [Orator, Law School students' association]).

Skinner, William F. 1986. "Delinquency, Crime and Development: A Case Study of Iceland." *Journal of Research in Crime and Delinquency* 23: 268–294.

State Alcohol and Tobacco Monopoly, annual reports. 1962, 1993, 1994. "Ársreikningar Áfengis- og tóbaksverslunar ríkisins." Reykjavík: ÁTVR.

State Criminal Investigative Police (SCIP), annual reports. 1991–1994. "Ársskýrslur Rannsóknarlögreglu ríkisins." Kópavogur.

Statistical Bureau of Iceland. 1992. Hagstofa Íslands. Unpublished information provided by the bureau. Reykjavík.

Steinsson, Steinn Kári. 1996. "Stefna íslenska ríkisvaldsins í áfengismálum" (Icelandic state policy on alcoholic beverages). B.A. thesis, University of Iceland.

Þjóðlíf. 1990. "Stóra, skrýtna kókaínmálið" (The big, strange cocaine case). Vol. 6, no. 4 (April): 8–12 (Reykjavík).

Þórðarson, Björn. 1926. *Refsivist á Íslandi 1761–1925* (Penal judgment completion in Iceland 1761–1925). Reykjavík: Gutenberg.

Þórlindsson, Þórólfur, and Jón Gunnar Bernburg. 1996. *Ofbeldi meðal íslenskra unglinga* (Violence among Icelandic adolescents). Reykjavík: Rannsóknastofnun uppeldis- og menntamála (Icelandic Institute for Education Research).

Þórmundsson, Jónatan. 1979. *Opinbert réttarfar* (Criminal justice), part 1. 2d ed. Reykjavík.

Þórmundsson, Jónatan. 1980. *Opinbert réttarfar* (Criminal justice), part 2. 2d ed. Reykjavík.

Þórmundsson, Jónatan. 1982. *Viðurlög við afbrotum* (Criminal punishment), part 1. Reykjavík.

Timberlake, James H. 1966. *Prohibition and the Progressive Movement: 1900–1920.* Cambridge, Mass.: Harvard University Press.

Tocqueville, Alexis de. [1835] 1956. *Democracy in America.* New York: Vintage Books.

Tomasson, Richard F. 1980. *Iceland: The First New Society.* Minneapolis, Minn.: University of Minnesota Press.

Traffic Council. 1988. Umferðaráð. "Skýrsla um umferðarslys á Íslandi, 1987" (Traffic related accidents in Iceland, 1987). Reykjavík.

Traffic Council. 1991. Umferðaráð. "Skýrsla um umferðarslys á Íslandi, 1990" (Traffic related accidents in Iceland, 1990). Reykjavík.

United States Department of Commerce. 1975. *Historical Statistics of the United States: Colonial Times to 1970.* Part 1. Washington, D.C.: Bureau of the Census.

Valsson, Karl Steinar. 1997. "Narkotikasituationen i Island" (The narcotics situation in Iceland). Pp. 95–109 in *Narkotikasituationen i Norden: Utvecklingen 1990–1996,* ed. Börje Olsson, Pia Rosenquist, and Anders Stymne. NAD publication no. 32. Helsinki: Nordic Council for Alcohol and Drug Research.

van den Hoonaard, Will C. 1991. "Nation's Innocence: Myth and Reality of Crime in Iceland." *Scandinavian-Canadian Studies* 4: 97–114.

Vísbending. 1994. "Er mikill tekjumunur á Íslandi?" (Is there a great income differential in Iceland?). Vol. 12, no. 44 (November 12) (Reykjavík; a weekly newsletter on business and economic affairs).

Vold, George. 1958. *Theoretical Criminology.* New York: Oxford University Press.

von Hofer, Hanns. 1990. "Homicide in Swedish Statistics, 1750–1988." Pp. 29–45 in vol. 11: *Criminal Violence in Scandinavia: Selected Topics,* ed. Annika Snare, of Scandinavian Studies in Criminology. Oslo: Norwegian University Press.

Weinberger, Eliot. 1997. "Paradise." *Nation,* 10 February: 36.

Wieting, Stephen G., and Þórólfur Þorlindsson. 1990. "Divorce in the Old Icelandic Commonwealth: An Interactionist Approach to the Past." *Studies in Symbolic Interactionism* 11: 163–189.

Williams, Kirk R., and Susan Drake. 1980. "Social Structure, Crime and Criminalization: An Empirical Examination of the Conflict Perspective." *Sociological Quarterly* 21: 563–575.

Wolf, Preben. 1971. "Crime and Development: An International Comparison of Crime Rates." Pp. 107–120 in vol. 3 of Scandinavian Studies in Criminology. Oslo: Scandinavian University Books.

World Drink Trends. 1996. *Produktschap voor gedistilleerde dranken.* Henley-on-Thames: NTC Publications.

Yearbook of Nordic Statistics. 1990. Vol. 28. Copenhagen: Nordic Council of Ministers and the Nordic Statistical Secretariat.

General Newspaper Articles

DV (Dagblaðið Vísir). 1977. "Meirihluti landsmanna hafnar bjórnum" (The majority of Icelanders opposes beer). 10 March, p. 8.

DV (Dagblaðið Vísir). 1984. "Afgerandi meirihluti vill þjóðaratkvæði um bjórinn" (The vast majority wants a national referendum on the issue of beer). 16 March, p. 4. Reykjavík.

Morgunblaðið. 1934. "Nýja bannið" (The new ban). 28 November, p. 3.

Morgunblaðið. 1953. "Verða ný áfengislög samþykkt á þessu þingi?" (New alcohol law passed in Parliament during this session?). 3 October, p. 8.

Morgunblaðið. 1960. "Bjór" (Beer). 12 November, p. 10.

Morgunblaðið. 1965a. "Ný ölgerð á Akureyri á næsta ári" (New brewery in Akureyri next year). 1 December, p. 32.

Morgunblaðið. 1965b. "Um öl" (On beer). 18 December, p. 14.

Morgunblaðið. 1966a. "Bjórinn" (The beer). 30 January, p. 6.

Morgunblaðið. 1966b. "721 millj. Carlsberg flöskur" (721 million bottles of Carlsberg beer). 18 February, p. 14.

Morgunblaðið. 1969a. "Dæmdur til að greiða nær 13 milljónir króna" (Convicted and to pay a fine of almost 13 million kronas). 22 January: p. 2.

Morgunblaðið. 1969b. "Stálu hljóðfærum" (Musical instruments stolen). 6 February, p. 24.

Morgunblaðið. 1969c. "Stal frystikistu ömmu sinnar" (Stole his grandmother's freezer). 25 March, p. 28.

Morgunblaðið. 1969d. "Ákærður fyrir 3ja milljóna króna tollsvik" (Charged for a 3 million kronas customs regulation forgery). 13 April, p. 2.

Morgunblaðið. 1969e. "Dæmdur í árs fangelsi" (Sentenced to one year prison). 20 June, p. 2.

Morgunblaðið. 1969f. "Flugvallarlögreglan fær prófunartæki til að finna hvort farþegar hafi eiturlyf meðferðis" (Airport police receives devices for drug search). 16 August, p. 3.

Morgunblaðið. 1969g. "Grunur á að unglingar neyti hassis" (Suspicion that adolescents use hashish). 9 October, p. 28.

Morgunblaðið. 1969h. "12 ára innbrotsþjófar í Keflavík og Njarðvík" (12-year-old burglars in Keflavík and Njarðvík). 25 October, p. 21.

Morgunblaðið. 1969i. "Unglingar uppvísir að neyslu nautnalyfja" (Adolescents found using drugs). 25 October, p. 32.

Morgunblaðið. 1969j. "Handtekin með sterk nautnalyf" (Arrested with hard drugs). 18 November, p. 32.

Morgunblaðið. 1969k. "Fíkniefnið rannsakað erlendis" (The drug's content determined abroad). 20 November, p. 31.

Morgunblaðið. 1969l. "Öll eiturlyf eru hættuleg" (All drugs are dangerous). 16 December, p. 16.

Morgunblaðið. 1969m. "Neysla ungra á eiturlyfjum" (Drug use among youth). 19 December, p. 32.

Morgunblaðið. 1974a. "Stórt fíkniefnamál í rannsókn" (A major drug case being investigated). 7 February, p. 35.

Morgunblaðið. 1974b. "Nauðgun og líkamsárásir" (Rape and assaults). 25 July, p. 3.

Morgunblaðið. 1974c. "Manns saknað í Keflavík" (Male is missing in Keflavík). 22 November, p. 2.

Morgunblaðið. 1974d. "Óvenju mikið um hvers kyns óhappaverk" (Unusually high number of various unfortunate deeds). 10 December, p. 48.

Morgunblaðið. 1979a. "Dæmdur í 2½ árs fangelsi í V-Þýskalandi vegna fíkniefna" (Sentenced to 2½ years in prison in West Germany for drugs). 2 January, p. 2.

Morgunblaðið. 1979b. "Landsbankamálið til saksóknara í dag: Ný gögn benda til að málið sé umfangsmeira og nái lengra aftur en talið var" (The Landsbanki case forwarded to the director of public prosecutions today: New evidence suggests that the case is more far-reaching than previously believed). 10 January, p. 32.

Morgunblaðið. 1979c. "Hassdómur í Þýskalandi: Íslendingur í 1 árs fangelsi" (Convicted for hashish in Germany: Icelander receives one year in prison). 16 January, p. 2.

Morgunblaðið. 1979d. "Ískyggileg fjölgun manndrápa hérlendis: 14 manndráp framin á síðustu sjö árum" (Terrifying increase of homicide cases in Iceland: 14 homicides committed in the past seven years). 18 January, p. 40.

Morgunblaðið. 1979e. "Ég skýt þig ef þú lætur mig ekki hafa alla peningana" (I will shoot you if you don't give me all the money). 1 February, p. 27.

Morgunblaðið. 1979f. "Íslendingar viðriðnir stærsta kókaínmál sem upp hefur komið" (Icelanders involved in the biggest cocaine case ever). 6 March, p. 3.

Morgunblaðið. 1979g. "Réttargæslumaður Íslendinganna: Málið ekki eins stórt og lögreglan telur" (The Icelanders' attorney: The case is not as big as the police believe). 8 March, pp. 22–23. (See also four other articles about this case on pp. 22–23 of this issue.)

Morgunblaðið. 1979h. "Tveir dæmdir fyrir nauðgun" (Two convicted of rape). 25 April, p. 2.

Morgunblaðið. 1979i. "Hlaut níu mánaða fangelsi fyrir ólöglega handtöku" (Sentenced to nine months in prison for an illegal arrest). 1 June, p. 32.

Morgunblaðið. 1979j. "Fíkniefnamál: Svíar vilja fá Íslending framseldan" (Drug case: Swedes request an Icelander to be extradited). 26 July, p. 36.

Morgunblaðið. 1979k. "Lést eftir ryskingar: Ungur maður í gæsluvarðhaldi" (Died after a brawl: Young man held in custody). 8 August, p. 40.

Morgunblaðið. 1979l. "Fíkniefnavandamálið verður sífellt alvarlegra: Ungmenni láta lífið vegna fíkniefnaneyslu"; continuation: "Heróín komið á markaðinn—4,000 ungmenni komið við sögu í fíkniefnamálum" (The drug problem is becoming increasingly serious: Young people die due to drug use. Heroin has made its entry to the market—4,000 young people have been involved in drug cases). 14 December, pp. 17, 32.

Morgunblaðið. 1983. "63.5% vilja leyfa sölu áfengs öls hjá ÁTVR" (A total of 63.5% favor beer sales in liquor stores). 20 November, p. 48.

Morgunblaðið. 1984a. "Þjóðarátak gegn ávana- og fíkniefnum" (National force against drugs). 7 January, p. 20.

Morgunblaðið. 1984b. "Fíkniefnalögreglan: Símar hleraðir í um 10 tilvikum á tveimur árum" (Drug police: Telephones have been tapped in about 10 cases in the last two years). 10 January, p. 2.

Morgunblaðið. 1984c. "39 ára kona fannst látin í íbúð við Njálsgötu" (39-year-old female found dead in Njalsgata apartment). 1 February, p. 32.

Morgunblaðið. 1984d. "Skaftamálið: Mál höfðað gegn lögregluþjónunum" (Case of Skafti: Police officers to be sued). 17 February, p. 2.

Morgunblaðið. 1984e. "Vopnaður maður rændi 1840 þúsundum króna frá ÁTVR" (An armed man robbed 1840 thousand kronas from a liquor store). 18 February, p. 48.

Morgunblaðið. 1984f. "Athvarf fyrir unga fíkniefnaneytendur?" (Emergency center for young drug users?). 4 March, pp. 38–39.

Morgunblaðið. 1984g. "Ofbeldi" (Violence). 15 March, p. 24.

Morgunblaðið. 1984h. "Furðulegar tillögur um aðgerðir í fíkníefnamálum" (Strange propositions on actions in drug cases). 27 March, p. 13.

Morgunblaðið. 1984i. Þýsk hjón handtekin með átta fálkaegg" (German couple apprehended with eight falcon eggs). 1 May, p. 32.

Morgunblaðið. 1984j. "Óður byssumaður í Vesturbænum í gærkveldi: Hótaði að drepa alla sem nálguðust hann" (Crazed gunman on the west side of town last night: Threatened to kill everyone who got close to him). 5 May, p. 48.

Morgunblaðið. 1984k. "Ríkissaksóknari:'Bjórlíki' allt annars eðlis en öl" (The state prosecutor declares that the so-called "beer" is different from beer). 10 May, p. 2.

Morgunblaðið. 1984l. "Andþingleg og ólýðræðisleg vinnubrögð" (Anti-parliamentarian and undemocratic conduct). 11 May, p. 7.

Morgunblaðið. 1984m. "Ríkissaksóknari kærir sakadómsúrskurð í nauðgunarmáli: Hæstiréttur úrskurði árásarmanninn í gæsluvarðhald" (Public prosecutions appeal a criminal court's decision in a rape case: Supreme Court to send attacker back into custody). 15 May, p. 2.

Morgunblaðið. 1984n. "Lögregla tók 700 grömm af amfetamíni og 400 af hassolíu: Söluverð fíkniefnanna 10 millj." (Police seized 700 grams of amphetamines and 400 of hashish oil). 30 May, pp. 22–23, 48.

Morgunblaðið. 1984o. "Ránið við Laugaveg 77: William Scobie fékk fimm ára fangelsisdóm: Vitorðsmaður fékk 18 mánuði og faðir Scobies 6 mánaða skilorðsbundinn dóm" (Robbery at Laugaveg 77: William Scobie sentenced to five years in prison: An accomplice got 18 months and Scobie's father, probation for 6 months). 28 June, p. 2.

Morgunblaðið. 1984p. "Athugasemd frá rannsóknarlögreglustjóra vegna fíkniefnamála" (Comment from chief of SCIP concerning drug cases). 5 July, p. 5.

Morgunblaðið. 1984q. "Rannsóknarlögregla ríkisins: Gæsluvarðhalds óskað eftir deilur nágranna" (State criminal investigative police: Custody requested after neighbors' quarrel). 21 August, p. 64.

Morgunblaðið. 1984r. "4 ára fangelsi fyrir nauðgun" (Four-year prison sentence for rape). 25 October, p. 3.

Morgunblaðið. 1984s. "10 ár frá hvarfi Geirfinns Einarssonar: Hinir dæmdu allir lausir" (Ten years from the disappearance of Geirfinnur Einarsson: Convicts have all been released). 18 November, p. 2.

Morgunblaðið. 1984t. "Mest traust á lögreglu—minnst á dagblöðunum" (Most confidence in the police—least in the press). 22 November, p. 36.

Morgunblaðið. 1984u. "Umfangsmesta LSD-mál hérlendis: 6 í haldi vegna LSD-smyglsins" (Largest case involving LSD ever: 6 in custody). 25 November, p. 2.

Morgunblaðið. 1987. "Alþingi: Fyrstu umræðu um bjórinn frestað í fjórða sinn" (Parliament: First round of debates on beer postponed for the fourth time). 25 November, p. 41.

Morgunblaðið. 1988. "Bjórfrumvarpið samþykkt í nótt" (The beer proposal was passed last night). 10 May, p. 72.

Morgunblaðið. 1989a. "Smyglaðferðir í fíkniefnamálum þróast: Hörð neysla lítt kortlögð utan mestu óregluhópa" (Methods of smuggling becoming more sophisticated: Use of hard drugs not mapped out, outside the group of reprobates). 12 February, p. 2.

Morgunblaðið. 1989b. "Tveir í gæsluvarðhaldi: Handteknir með kókaín í Miðbænum" (Two in custody: Arrested with cocaine in the downtown area). 21 February, p. 2.

Morgunblaðið. 1989c. "Hald lagt á 700 LSD skammta" (700 doses of LSD seized). 25 April, p. 48.

Morgunblaðið. 1989d. "Tveir menn í gæsluvarðhaldi: Umfangsmesta fíkniefnamál hérlendis" (Two men in custody: Biggest drug case ever). 18 May, p. 2.

Morgunblaðið. 1989e. "Fundu 4–5 kíló af hassi" (4–5 kilos of hashish seized). 24 May, p. 44.

Morgunblaðið. 1989f. "Sakadómur: 6 mánaða fangelsisvist fyrir hórmang" (Criminal court: Six-month prison sentence for pimping). 14 October, p. 44.

Morgunblaðið. 1989g. "Lögreglustjórinn í Reykjavík: Sum svæði ekki örugg um helgar" (Police chief of Reykjavík: Some areas not safe on weekends). 3 December, p. 36.

Morgunblaðið. 1989h. "Níu kærur til lögreglu vegna líkamsmeiðinga um helgina: Tveir menn hlutu alvarlega áverka í átökum" (Nine reports of violence to police over the weekend: Two men seriously injured after a brawl). 5 December, p. 2.

Morgunblaðið. 1989i. "Borgarráð krefst tafarlausra úrbóta í löggæslumálum" (City council demands immediate control actions). 6 December, p. 2.

Morgunblaðið. 1989j. "Látinn laus eftir sjö mánaða gæsluvarðhald" (Released after seven months in custody). 8 December, p. 2.

Morgunblaðið. 1989k. "Hugmyndir um úrbætur í miðbæ Reykjavíkur um helgar: Myndavélar til eftirlits og lögregla með hunda" (Suggestions of actions to be taken in downtown Reykjavík on weekends: Cameras to be installed and police officers patrol with dogs). 12 December, p. 4.

Morgunblaðið. 1991. "Arfleifð einvaldskonunganna kvödd" (Farewell to the legacy of monarchy). 6 October, pp. 25–27.

Morgunblaðið. 1992a. "Lögreglumaður í lífshættu" (Police officer's life in danger). 18 August, p. 52.

Morgunblaðið. 1992b. "Rétt staðið að verki við eftirförina og farið eftir reglum" (The car chase was in accordance with proper police conduct and regulations). 19 August, p. 21.

Morgunblaðið. 1992c. "5–10 stórneytendur kókaíns greinast árlega á Vogi" (5–10 heavy users of cocaine diagnosed each year at Vog Rehab). 20 August, pp. 20–21.

Morgunblaðið. 1993a. "Héraðsdómur Reykjavíkur: Átján mánaða fangelsi 20 dögum eftir afbrot" (Reykjavík's criminal court: Eighteen-month prison sentence 20 days after crime). 14 January, p. 2.

Morgunblaðið. 1993b. "Dómur Héraðsdóms í fíkniefnamáli: Tvítugir bræður voru dæmdir í tólf mánaða fangelsi" (Criminal's court decision in a drug case: Twenty-year-old brothers sentenced to twelve months in prison). 27 January, p. 2.

Morgunblaðið. 1993c. "Fjölmennt í Kvennaathvarfinu: Helmingi fleiri konur nú í janúar en í fyrra" (Crowded in the women's center: Number of women admitted in January has doubled since last year). 3 February, p. 2.

Morgunblaðið. 1993d. "Fimm ára fangelsi fyrir manndrápstilraun" (Five-year prison sentence for attempted manslaughter). 12 February, p. 25.

Morgunblaðið. 1993e. "Afbrotafaraldur" (Crime epidemic). 7 March, p. 26.

Morgunblaðið. 1993f. "Hundruða milljóna tjón í innbrotum" (Hundreds of millions lost because of burglaries). 13 March, p. 3.

Morgunblaðið. 1993g. "4 ára fangelsi og 500 þús. kr. sekt: Staðfestur dómur í málningarfötumáli" (4 year prison and 500 thousand kronas fine: A court decision confirmed in the case of paint cans). 2 April, p. 2.

Morgunblaðið. 1993h. "Tekinn með 20 millj. virði af amfetamín" (Arrested with amphetamines worth 20 million kronas). 21 April, p. 48.

Morgunblaðið. 1993i. "Héraðsdómur dæmir mann fyrir 2 nauðganir, árás og rán: 10 ára fangelsi og 2 milljónir í skaðabætur" (Criminal court convicts a male for 2 rapes, an assault and a robbery: 10-year prison sentence and 2 million kronas compensation). 8 May, p. 2.

Morgunblaðið. 1993j. "Eiturlyf og afbrot—orsök og afleiðing" (Drugs and crime—cause and consequence). 12 May, p. 22.

Morgunblaðið. 1993k. "Rannsóknaraðferðir innan eðlilegra marka" (Investigative methods within reasonable limits). 22 May, p. 25.

Morgunblaðið. 1993l. "Áverkum eftir ofbeldi fjölgað um 20 prósent frá 1980: Áverkar á brjóstholi og kvið stöðugt algengari" (Wounds inflicted by violence increased by 20 percent since 1980: Wounds on breast and stomach increasingly common). 1 December, p. 24.

Index

instrumental legislation, 29, 30, 31, 43, 44, 87

jury system, 110, 112, 113

Keflavík, 35, 52, 53, 58, 96, 97, 102, 106, 146
Kópavogur, 117, 118, 123, 124
Kvíabryggja, 117, 118, 125, 127

Litla-Hraun, 117, 118, 119–121, 125, 129, 131, 133, 136
LSD, 51, 53, 56, 57, 92, 95, 127

mass media, 3, 4, 7, 11, 34, 38, 48, 52, 53, 54, 58, 59, 60, 61, 62, 63, 67, 71, 80, 82, 94, 115, 131, 142, 143, 145, 148. *See also Morgunblaðið*
Morgan, Patricia A., 30, 43
Morgunblaðið, 16, 33, 34, 35, 36, 37, 38, 39, 45, 48, 49, 54, 94, 97, 98, 100

Nadelmann, Ethan A., 92, 93
Norway, 14, 110

parole and probation, 25, 56, 116, 124, 128, 133
police, 4, 7, 12, 23, 25, 27, 39, 51, 53, 54, 55, 56, 57, 58, 78, 79, 81, 82, 85, 86, 87, 92–102, 105–108, 109, 111, 112, 114, 115, 117, 124, 128, 129, 138, 140, 142, 147. *See also* drug police
Prison and Probation Administration, 25, 116, 118, 129, 135–136
prison population, 22, 23, 27, 116, 119, 121, 124, 125, 129, 131, 133, 136, 138, 139, 141, 142, 143, 148. *See also* inmates
prison terms, 25, 49, 52, 54, 55, 57, 58, 92, 97, 101, 118, 119, 121, 122, 124, 125, 128, 133, 135, 141
Progressive Party, 39, 46
property crime, 19, 21, 23, 27, 49, 51, 52, 53, 55, 57, 58, 59, 60, 67, 75, 107, 108, 122, 124, 125, 131, 135, 136, 137, 138, 139, 141
punishment, 7, 8, 9, 10, 11, 15, 62, 67, 75, 80, 82, 83, 84, 89, 122, 125, 135, 143, 144, 146, 147, 148

Quinney, Richard, 7, 139, 145

Rape Report, 12, 54, 55, 67, 81–90, 99, 144
recidivism, 71, 86, 108, 109, 118, 121, 124, 126, 129, 131, 133, 136
rehabilitation, 25, 81, 89, 98, 122, 125, 133, 135, 144
repressive sanctioning, 143
restitutive sanctioning, 143–144
Reykjavík, 12, 13, 23, 27, 34, 38, 39, 40, 46, 51, 55, 56, 57, 58, 80, 81, 98, 105, 106, 107, 111, 113, 114, 117, 118, 123, 125, 129, 131, 138, 142
rural areas, 12, 43, 52, 53, 66, 67, 68, 69, 70, 72, 73, 74, 78, 79, 114, 126, 137, 176, 181, 182, 217, 225
Russell, Diane, 84, 86

sex crimes, 7, 12, 13, 16, 20, 21, 22, 49, 52, 54, 55, 57, 58, 61, 67, 71, 81–91, 99, 107, 131, 137–138, 139, 143, 144, 145
socialist parties, 39, 42, 46
social stratification, 9, 15, 31, 75, 145
State Criminal Investigative Police (SCIP), 23, 54, 71, 84, 85, 90, 93, 94, 99, 106, 107, 108, 111, 114
state police, 23, 106, 114
status conflict, 30, 43, 44
Supreme Court, 49, 52, 58, 93, 94, 98, 100, 112
Sweden, 12, 14, 54
Switzerland, 3–5, 12, 18, 19, 59, 140, 141–143
symbolic legislation, 29–31, 41, 43, 44, 47, 87

Tocqueville, Alexis de, 112
Tomasson, Richard, 5, 6, 8, 9, 22, 43

undercover techniques, 56, 92, 93
unemployment, 6, 9, 96, 102, 103, 138, 139, 145
United Kingdom, 10, 30, 31, 36, 84, 110, 112, 113, 140
United States, 7, 10, 18, 29, 30, 31, 34, 39, 41, 42, 43, 51, 57, 61, 67, 75, 78, 79, 84, 92, 93, 100, 102, 103, 106, 107, 112, 113, 116, 140, 145